In the name of God, Most Gracious, Most Merciful

Read, in the name of your Lord, who created.
He created man from an embryo.
Read, and your Lord, Most Exalted.
Teaches by means of the pen.
He teaches man what he never knew.
(Quran: 96:1-5)

SELF-KNOWLEDGE
AND
SPIRITUAL YEARNING

*The Role of Spirituality
in Psychological Health*

E. Douglass Brown, PhD.

Key Concepts Institute
via Parchment Global Publishing
244 Fifth Avenue, Suite V278,
New York, N.Y. 10001
www.parchmentglobalpublishing.com

ISBN: 978-1-957009-10-0 (sc)
ISBN: 978-1-957009-09-4 (hc)
ISBN: 978-1-957009-08-7 (e)

Library of Congress Control Number: 2022903246

CONTENTS

Preface

All that is said and written about personality is not equal in accuracy, depth, or focus. An individual just learning to drive does not ask someone who has poor driving skills to teach him or her how to drive. A mature individual questions a medical diagnosis if the diagnosis was made by a physician who had never met the individual and only had scant knowledge about the individual's medical history. When it comes to the most important aspect of human nature—*the unique self*—most individuals rely on others to tell them who and what they are, where they came from, where they are going, why they do what they do, and what makes them individuals. While philosophers, psychologists, psychiatrists, and historians convey important information about human experience, the information is incomplete and inaccurate in some aspects. Through introspection and sharing experiences and knowledge with relatives, friends, students, clients, and colleagues for three decades, I fully recognize an overarching theme underlying human experience. People seek inner solace, peace of mind, and self-knowledge. Most people are intuitively aware that achieving authentic lasting inner solace and peace, and self-realization involves connecting with the Spiritual Reality behind all things.

The relationship between personality development, psychospiritual well-being, and God-consciousness has always been of deep value to the faithful among humanity. Despite pervasive assaults of materialism, secularism, and atheism in the last two centuries, the inherent human yearning for spiritual realization has not abated. The idea that spirituality has no place in personality development is baseless. The qualitative absence of a healthy spiritual orientation motivates many people to search for philosophies of life that they deem to be greater than themselves, and all they can achieve and accumulate. The search has been costly for those who do not understand the relationship between what they view as separate spheres of life—*the spiritual quest and self-development.*

There is ample experiential and scientific evidence that human beings are hardwired for a spiritual quest. Over the ages, thousands of seekers, sages, and scientists have confirmed the relationship, and individuals who acknowledge this truth probe further into the relationship between personality and spirituality. As a psychospiritual creature, a human being is more than his or her physical carriage that consists of a body, brain, senses, and appetites. Comprehensive approaches to the study of personality include the significance of the spiritual dimension.

To deny or discount the Divine origin and purpose of humanity is to write off *fundamental human psychospiritual characteristics*. As a consequence of ignoring the characteristics and relegating inquiries about them to philosophers and theologians, contemporary psychology has presented an ideal personality that is devoid of spirit, absolved of spiritual faith and ambition, and absent an integrated well-being.

My understanding of the interconnectedness of personality development and the spiritual quest is rooted in lessons learned on my own spiritual journey, invaluable counsel from life teachers, formal academic training in psychology, three decades of clinical observations as a clinical psychologist of hundreds of people from different cultures and backgrounds in inpatient and outpatient settings, and service as a college teacher and consultant. Most importantly, I evaluate tenets of psychology in the light of confirmed Divine guidance. This orientation is deemed strange and "unscientific" in the eyes of many mental health professionals and laypersons nested in a materialistic ultra-secular psychology. The limited materialistic secular view does not traditionally admit to the existence of a Supreme Being. Inspired to move beyond those limits before completing graduate school, I searched for irrefutable truths about personality development and psychological functioning. Human information about human nature and psychology is incomplete and always subject to error. To acquire a thorough understanding of personality and self-development, a person must also examine truths revealed in confirmed Divine scripture. There is no better source of information about fundamentals of mental health and personality development than the Architect of human consciousness and personality.

Your Lord is fully aware of your innermost thoughts. If you maintain righteousness, He is Forgiver of those who repent. (17:25)

We created the human, and we know what he whispers to himself. We are closer to him than his jugular vein. (50:16)

Does he [human] think that no one sees him? (90:7)

In *Self-Knowledge and Spiritual Yearning,* I introduce readers to elements of personality development delineated in the Divinely revealed scripture known as the *Quran.* My "reconnaissance map" in life, the Quran is a wellspring of information about personality development, self-awareness, mental health, and psychopathology. The content of the Quran's verses and the arrangement of its written text have been subjected to rigorous *scientific* scrutiny.[1] The Quran contains information about the physical universe (e.g., the Big Bang) and phenomena on earth that were unknown at the time the Quran was revealed. Mankind later understood numerous phenomena mentioned in the Quran only after the advent of modern science. The discovery thirty-three years ago of a miraculous mathematical system embedded in the text of the Quran confirms that God authored the Quran.[2]

In the West, readers have access to numerous works about religious and cultural perspectives of self-development. This has not been the case with respect to the Quran and Islam as delineated in the Quran. In *Self-Knowledge and Spiritual Yearning,* readers have an opportunity to learn about the Islamic science of the self (*An-Naf'saniya*), and the Islamic science of personality (*Ash-Shakh'saniya).* In the Quran, no distinction is made between spiritual growth and personality development. A closer examination of the word *psyche* reflects the fact that personality development includes spiritual growth. In the Oxford American Desk Dictionary,[3] *psyche* means "soul, spirit, and mind." *Spirit* means "soul; a person's mental nature or qualities." The term *psychospiritual* (*ruhiya*) encompasses crucial elements of both concepts and reflects the fact that a person's psycho-emotional life cannot be adequately understood when it is viewed as independent of his or her spiritual condition. This book orients students of the mind and self-discovery to elements of personality development that are unknown, frequently misunderstood, and missing from annals of traditional psychology.

This completely revised edition of *Self-Knowledge and Spiritual Yearning* features more information from the Quran and new scientific findings. The coupling of scientific findings about human consciousness and personality development with verses from the Quran erases doubt that self-development *is* spiritual healing. This edition includes confirmation of the presence of order and design underpinning life in this world. Comprehensive and accurate explanations of personality development acknowledge the order, the design, and the Author of the order and design. A person's decision about whether or not to grow his or her soul is at the heart of what it means to be a human being—a creature endowed with higher consciousness and a free will to think, reflect, and take safe harbor in his or her own vision of truth. Healthy personality development and self-knowledge are fruits of an innate guided spiritual yearning (*shawq ur-ruhi*). From the Quranic perspective, genuine human affirmation of the existence of God represents the epitome of human character. The affirmation is submission of the created (human) spirit mind to God, the Absolute Divine Spirit Mind. The heart of personality is the yearning for the Absolute Spirit Mind. A person who ignores the heart of personality cannot attain self-knowledge or experience the supreme rapture that engulfs actualized souls.

E. Douglass Brown

1

Humankind On The Great Chain Of Being

Personality development is the conscientious process of becoming the true self, a process that is part of a Divine system of reunion with the Absolute One. No individual can know who he or she really is unless that individual seeks and heeds the Absolute One who created all things. Human life is an opportunity for each person to discover his or her real self and life purpose.

> Man's main task in life is to give birth to himself, to become what he potentially is. The most important product of his effort is his own personality.[4]

Amidst life's vicissitudes, one chooses to pursue the True Reality or to become enveloped in veils of the physical senses and appetites. Self-imposed entrapment in sensory experience prevents a person from recognizing his or her true transcendent self. Through seeking the True Reality, a person comes to know why he or she is stationed in this world. A conscientious person who carefully reads authentic passages from revealed scripture learns that all humans are souls that existed before their individual births into this life. Each person has the opportunity to *evolve inwardly* and grow as a psychospiritual being.

> *The human being asks, "After I die, do I come back to life?" Did the human being forget that we created him already, and he was nothing? (19:66-67)*

> *God created the heavens and the earth for a specific purpose, in order to pay each soul for whatever it earned, without the least injustice.(45:22)*

> *I did not create the jinns and the humans except to worship Me alone. (51:56)*

He created the heavens and the earth for a specific purpose, designed you and perfected your design, then to Him is the final destiny.(64:3)

Inspired by the words of the Quran, an ancient fraternity of Seekers of Purity and Truth known as the Ikhwan Al-Safa wrote:

Everything exists for a purpose, the final purpose of the cosmos being the return of multiplicity to Unity…*there is no question of an indefinite gradation of physical forms.* Once the origin has been reached again, there is no further step to be taken…In the perfect man who has realized his Divine origin the process has come to an end. *Man's evolution is therefore inward;* God does not create something after man as He created man after the animals, because man, by virtue of being able to return to his origin, fulfills the purpose of the whole creation. All other orders of beings were created in order that this final stage of reunion might take place.[5]

Modern science has liberated the willing from a *tema ridiculum*, the absurd idea that humans evolved from primate apes and by random forces. Desperate to cloak humanity's origin in the ragtag garment of evolution, some intellectuals and laypersons sacrifice their minds on an altar of "lame science."[6] The eminent zoologist and biologist Dr. Edwin Conklin[7] (1863-1952) was a professor at Ohio Wesleyan University, Northwestern University, University of Pennsylvania, and Princeton University. At the invitation of President Woodrow Wilson, Dr. Conklin was named the first full time Chairperson of the Princeton University Department of Biology. Regarding evolution, Dr. Conklin said:

The probability of life originating from accident is comparable to the probability of the unabridged dictionary resulting from an explosion in a printing shop."[8]

Irrefutable *scientific* findings coupled with miraculous code-based Quran verses further prove that evolutionary theory is untenable *as an explanation of the origin of life.* In clarifying elements of psychospiritual growth and personality development, it is first important to remove the mask of evolution that has covered man's true countenance for 148 years. Many mainstream Western theories of personality development were formulated on the theses that humans evolved from apes and life is by chance. The Quranic perspective of personality does not rest on these bogus notions.

Physical Evolution Does Not Apply

For eons, men have pondered and reflected on our origins. Some have held that we originated in the sands and clay beneath our feet. Others believe that celestial relatives placed our first parents on earth as orphans. Some believe that we are the descendents of primate pioneers. Though full of intrigue, mystery, and fodder for movies and books, these scenarios are false. The rhetoric about a primate pioneer of humans lingers on. Far from science, the rhetoric appeals to minds thirsting to be regarded as well-informed, realistic, and objective. The rhetoric also comforts individuals eager to commandeer new recruits to search for evidence of ape-human evolution. In the recruiters' minds, the search is equivalent to the truism that ape-man evolution is plausible. The search is akin to the quest of a deluded treasure hunter who, despite clear and mounting evidence that a sought-after treasure is non-existent, feels compelled to continue looking for it. Constantly attempting to convince others that treasure is buried beneath the surface, the hunter says, "Keep looking! Keep digging…we'll eventually find it!" When questioned about his incessant digging, the treasure hunter says, "I cannot stop. If I stop digging, *I* stop. All that I believe about life's purpose hinges on finding the treasure!" Some authors continue to assert that there is an infinite evolutionary gradation of physical forms leading to the human being.[9] For example, the authors of a text on personality published in 1975 stated:

> *Australopithecus*, the first step in human evolution, was a small apelike creature, a vegetarian living in wooded areas and limited to near-tropical regions… *Australopithecus* and the millions of humans who followed them migrated in responses to environmental demands.[10]

In a 2003 *Edmonton Sun* newspaper article, Ted Byfield reported that:

> If parents check the science textbooks used in Canadian schools they'll see some familiar illustrations, familiar because much the same art appeared in their textbook. There's the "evolution of man" illustration, starting with an ape-like creature on the left, then progressing to the slightly more erect

figure with arms stretching to the ground, then to a less hairy individual, finally to a modern human…. This fall there has appeared a scientifically authoritative book casting grave doubt on the whole basis of these confident illustrations. Dr. Jonathan Wells, a molecular and cell biologist from the University of California at Berkeley who is a senior fellow of the Discovery Institute, in his *Icons of Evolution,* does more than cast doubt…. He takes 10 so-called "proofs" of evolution offered in current textbooks and shows where not one of them is in fact a proof of anything, and several are actually frauds. The speckled moths were actually pasted on the trees, not found there. And while there may be rare instances of species that seem part ape, part human, there is no evidence the one came from the other.[11]

In his 2003 *National Review* article, "Darwin in the Classroom," John G. West, Jr. wrote:

Thanks to the book *Icons of Evolution* by biologist Jonathan Wells, more people know about how biology textbooks perpetuate discredited "icons" of evolution that many biologists no longer accept as good science. Embryo drawings purporting to prove Darwin's theory of common ancestry continue to appear in many textbooks despite the embarrassing fact that they have been exposed as fakes originally concocted by 19th-century German Darwinist Ernst Haeckel. Textbooks likewise continue to showcase microevolution in peppered moths as evidence for Darwin's mechanism of natural selection even though the underlying research is now questioned by many biologists.[12]

The authors of a 1976 biology text for social science students suggested that the concept of special creation is contrary to rational scientific inquiry:

Such a concept of special creation by a supernatural force is outside the realm of science because it is simply not possible to test its validity by scientific methods…The scientist, on the other hand, must seek a rational explanation that will be consistent with what is known about natural forces and with established scientific principles.[13]

Based on what is known about DNA and the genetic blueprint of life, it is illogical to conclude that the idea of special creation is outside the realm of science. Based on such a conclusion, *any* phenomena deemed "special" (i.e., uncountable or unobservable) must prima facie be considered unworthy of study. *The Quran and other authentic revealed scriptures do not contradict scientific facts.* However, some individuals believe that they do not have sufficient *external* information to conclude that some phenomenon revealed in Divine scriptures are facts. Synonymous with truth and reality, facts are independent of man's conclusions about whether they are true. The scientific method cannot *determine* if something is a fact. The method is a systematic process of observation, investigation, and study. Science and the scientific method do not rule out the special creation of humans. *People* decided to rule out special creation. Proper use of the scientific method is indispensable for open-minded individuals to objectively investigate any area that interests them. Science stresses the objective organized pursuit of all knowledge within human reach. On innumerable occasions, scientific research findings support truths revealed in authentic scripture. On the other hand, some individuals (not science) argue that if a phenomenon or event noted in authentic scripture has not been "scientifically validated," it is not true. Credible scientists do not deny alternative plausible explanations when their own explanations are proved incorrect. According to the Quran, the origin of life can be deciphered by studying fossils and skeletal remains of early life forms.[14]

> *Have they not seen how God initiates the creation, then repeats it? This is easy for God to do. Say, "Roam the earth and find out the origin of life." For God will thus initiate the creation in the Hereafter. God is Omnipotent (29:19-20)*

Mechanics and Complexity of Biological Life Point to God

By studying fossils, the skeletal remains of early life forms, and cell structure, scientists see *how* God initiates and repeats the physical creation. For example, the difference between the number and type of DNA nucleotide structures in apes and in humans is so great that an ape-to-human link is impossible. A noted molecular biologist, Dr. Michael Denton (1996) observed that:

> In all organisms the roles of DNA, mRNA and protein are identical. The meaning of the genetic code is also virtually identical in all cells. The size, structure and component design of the protein synthetic machinery is practically the same in all cells. In terms of the basic biochemical design, therefore no living system can be thought of as being primitive or ancestral with respect to any other system, nor is there the slightest empirical hint of

an evolutionary sequence among all the incredibly diverse cells on earth. For those who hoped that molecular biology might bridge the gulf between chemistry and biochemistry, the revelation was profoundly disappointing.[15]

Dr. Denton also pointed out that the composition of a single cell reflects a degree of sophistication and order that supersedes anything that man can fashion.

The complexity of the simplest known type of cell is so great that it is impossible to accept that such an object could have been thrown together by some kind of freakish, vastly improbable event. Such an occurrence would be indistinguishable from a miracle…It is astonishing to think that this remarkable piece of machinery, which possesses the ultimate capacity to construct every living thing that *ever* existed on earth…can construct all of its own components in a matter of minutes and weigh less than 10-16 grams. It is of the order of several thousand million times smaller than the smallest piece of functional machinery ever constructed by man.[16]

Recently discovered biochemical and genetic evidence of order and design is not hypothetical nor does it rest on unproved assumptions. Effective municipal operations require ongoing direction, management, maintenance, organization, communication, structure, and planning. Operations in a single cell are comparable to the work required to run a city.[17] The proteins are the workers. The mitochondria that convert food into energy are the power plants. The actin fibers and microtubules are the roads, and the kinesin and dynein that transport "cellular cargo" along microtubules are the trucks. The ribosomes are the factories. The genome, that contains DNA and RNA, is the library where all the information about the city is kept. The lysosomes that digest waste and bacteria are the recycling center. The chaperones that assist other proteins amidst cellular stress are the police department. The Golgi Apparatus that processes and packages protein and lipids is the post office.

Regarding physical evidence of human evolution, John Reader comments:

The entire hominid (a so-called 'ape-man' fossil) collection known today would barely cover a billiard table…. Ever since Darwin…preconceptions have led evidence by the nose in the study of fossil man.[18]

Dr. Wolfgang Smith who holds doctoral degrees in mathematics and physics, stated:

[N]ow that the actual physical structure of what might be termed the biochemical mainstays of life [DNA] has come into view, scientists are finding—frequently to their dismay—that the evolutionist thesis has become more stringently unthinkable than ever before…[O]n the molecular level, these separations and this hierarchic order stand out with a mathematical precision which once and for all silences dissent. On the fundamental level it becomes a rigorously demonstrable fact that there are no transitional types, and that the so-called missing links are indeed non-existent.[19]

Some proponents of ape-to-human evolution frequently state that humans share 98 percent of their genes with apes. To a person uninformed about the nature and structure of genes, such a statement may sound consistent with ape-to-human evolution. However, some proponents fail to inform their audiences that many creatures share nearly the same amount of genome nucleotides. Dr. Lisa Stubbs points out in her article "How Closely Related Are Mice and Humans?" that:

Mice and humans (indeed, most or all mammals including dogs, cats, rabbits, monkeys, and apes) have roughly the same number of nucleotides in their genomes—about 3 billion base pairs. This comparable DNA content implies that all mammals contain more or less the same number of genes, and indeed our work and the work of many others have provided evidence to confirm that notion…However, the most significant differences between mice and humans are not in the number of genes each carries but in the structure of genes and the activities of their protein products… The often-quoted statement that we share over 98% of our genes with apes (chimpanzees, gorillas, and orangutans) actually should be put another way. That is, there is more than 95% to 98% similarity between related genes in humans and apes in general. (Just as in the mouse, quite a few genes probably are not common to humans and apes, and these may influence uniquely human or ape traits.) Similarities between mouse and human genes range from about 70% to 90%, with an average of 85% similarity but a lot of variation from gene to gene (e.g., some mouse and human gene products are almost identical, while others are nearly unrecognizable as close relatives).[20]

In his article, "The Human Genome Revealed," Dr. David Plaisted notes that a large variation in life forms proceeds from a few genes.

> Even if all of the human genes were different from those of a chimpanzee, the DNA could still be 98.5 percent similar if the noncoding DNA of humans and chimpanzees was identical. Of course, human and chimpanzee genes probably are similar, but the degree of similarity cannot be estimated from the overall DNA similarity…The smaller number of genes does make it easier to imagine apes and humans having a common ancestor 5 or 10 million years ago, since the smaller genome can tolerate a higher mutation rate without error catastrophe. But the number of genes may still be too large…If the number of genes really turns out to be about 30,000, then this can be a testament to the marvelous design of life. *Only a genius could create us with so few genes performing so many functions.*[21] (italics added)

In contrast to Plaisted's "genius," some individuals argue that the human species resulted from a random series of genetic mutations. In the twenty-first century, making this argument requires dismissing key information about the structure of the DNA double helix.

> DNA Double Helix: Its Existence Alone Defeats Any Theory of Evolution
> The scientific reality of the DNA double helix can single-handedly defeat any theory that assumes life arose from non-life through materialistic forces. Evolution theory has convinced many people that the design in our world is merely "apparent"—just the result of random, natural processes. However, with the discovery, mapping, and sequencing of the DNA molecule, we now understand that organic life is based on a vastly complex information code, and such information cannot be created or interpreted without a Master Designer at the cosmic keyboard.[22]

In March 2006, NASA scientists discovered a nebula in the shape of a DNA Double Helix, located in the center of the Milky Way galaxy.

> Magnetic forces at the center of the galaxy have twisted a nebula into the shape of DNA, a new study reveals. The double helix shape is commonly seen inside living organisms, but this is the first time it has been observed in the cosmos. "Nobody has ever seen anything like that before in the

cosmic realm," said the study's lead author Mark Morris of UCLA…What we see indicates a high degree of order." The DNA nebula is about 80 light-years long. It's about 300 light-years from the supermassive black hole at the center of the Milky Way. The nebula is nearly perpendicular to the black hole, moving out of the galaxy at a quick clip—about 620 miles per second (1,000 kilometers per second)… It's like having two strands of rope connected to a fixed point, Morris said. As you spin the strands, they braid around each other in a double helix fashion. In this case the gas and dust of the nebula makes up the strands…This process takes a long time, though, since the disk completes one orbit around the black hole roughly every 10,000 years. But that's an important number. "Once every 10,000 years is exactly what we need to explain the twisting of the magnetic field lines that we see in the double helix nebula," Morris said.[23]

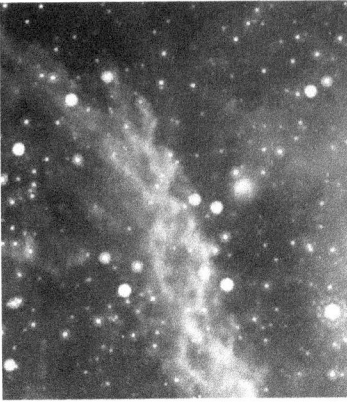

Figure 1.1. DNA Helix Nebula.

NASA Spitzer Space Telescope photograph of "DNA nebula" at the center of the Milky Way galaxy, on March 15, 2006. This is an example of the same complexity, design, and order in the macrocosm (cosmos) as is found in the microcosm (molecule).

(Source:http://www.space.com)

The 10,000 year-old DNA nebula at the center of the Milky Way galaxy mirrors the DNA double Helix shape in the center of cells in living organisms. This proves that *the Master Designer of cellular DNA is the Master Designer of the cosmos.* In contrast to the 10,000 years it took for the DNA nebula to form, it takes a few minutes for the same designed structure and pattern to emerge in a cell. The time difference in the formation of the DNA nebula and the formation of a biological cell is an example that the creation of the universe was far more 'difficult' than the creation of the human being (79:27-28). This intricate structure and pattern in both the macrocosm and the microcosm is not a coincidence.

We will show them our proofs in the horizons, and within themselves, until they realize that this is the truth. Is your Lord not sufficient as a witness of all things? (41:53)

He is the One God; the Creator, the Initiator, the Designer. To Him belong the most beautiful names. Glorifying Him is everything in the heavens and the earth. He is the Almighty, Most Wise. (59:24)

He created the heavens and the earth for a specific purpose, designed you and perfected your design, then to Him is the final destiny. (64:3)

Are you more difficult to create than the heaven? He constructed it. He raised its masses, and perfected it. (79:27-28)

The One who created you, designed you, and perfected you. (82:7)

The author and biochemist, Dr. Michael J. Behe, makes this point:

[I]nferring that biochemical systems were designed by an intelligent agent is a humdrum process that requires no new principles of logic or science. It comes simply from the hard work that biochemistry has done over the past forty years, combined with consideration of the way in which we reach conclusions of design every day.[24]

The fact of *irreducible complexity* has completely dispelled the notion that all life proceeded from a simple cell. In his book, *Darwin's Black Box*, Dr. Behe points out that a simple cell is composed of highly complex basic components that could not have emerged independent of each other. Basic components necessary for cellular functioning *must be present at the same time, operational, and correctly bonded.* Dr. Behe wrote:

By *irreducibly complex* I mean a single system composed of several well-matched, interacting parts that contribute to the basic function, wherein the removal of any one of the parts causes the system to effectively cease functioning. An irreducibly complex system cannot be produced directly (that is, by continuously improving the initial function, which continues to work by the same mechanism) by slight, successive modifications of a precursor system, because any precursor to an irreducibly complex system that is missing a part is by definition nonfunctional. An irreducibly complex biological system, if there is such a thing, would be a powerful challenge to Darwinian evolution.[25]

The fact that evolution is a myth is further indicated when data is presented about the mathematical improbability of such a phenomena. The authors of the article, "DNA and Cells," quote non-creationist scientists regarding such a process.

Chance is not good enough. Every protein must have its amino acids in the proper amount and order. Yet there are 2,500,000,000,000,000,000 different ways that the 20 basic amino acids can be arranged. Get just one out of order, and death or serious damage will result to the organism... According to evolutionary theory, every aspect of a person's structure and function came about by chance—till just the right one was hit upon. How long would you live, if you had to wait 20 billion years for each of your millions of proteins to be developed by chance?—*pp.29-30.* **Dixon-Webb calculation.** Two evolutionists estimated that, in order to get the needed amino acids in close enough proximity to form a given protein molecule, a rich mixture of already formed amino acids, with a total volume equal to 10^{50} times the volume of our earth would be needed.—*p.31.***Computer simulation.** A gathering of leading scientists met, in 1967, at the Wistar Institute. Schutzenberger, a computer scientist, explained to them that the entire evolutionary process had been fed into computers and simulated. He announced that, mathematically, it had proven to be totally impossible for evolution to occur.—*pp. 32-33.*[26] (page notations are part of quote)

More than eighty-seven years ago, scientists in America realized that the existence of an Intelligent Being or God could be proven through chemistry. Thomas Edison, the inventor of the electric light bulb and phonograph, gave the following response to questions posed to him about the existence of an Intelligent Creator:

Atoms in harmonious and useful relation assume beautiful or interesting shapes and colors.... [G]athered together in certain forms, the atoms [or elements] constitute animals of the lower order. Finally, they combine in man, who represents the total intelligence of all the atoms. "From where does this intelligence come from originally?" asked the interviewer. "From some power greater than ourselves," answered Edison. "Do you believe, then, in an intelligent Creator, a personal God?" "Certainly. The existence of such a God can, to my mind, be proved from chemistry."[27]

One of the greatest scientist of the twentieth century and discoverer of the Law of Relativity, Dr. Albert Einstein said,

> The source of all scientific advancement is the *God-given curiosity* [italics added] of the toiling experimenter and the constructive fantasy of the technical inventor…. The basis of all scientific work is the conviction that the world is an ordered and comprehensive entity, which *is a* religious sentiment. My religious feeling is a humble amazement at the order revealed in the small patch of reality to which our feeble intelligence is equal.[28]

Einstein pointed out that,

> If a person were hurled at the velocity of light [186,000 miles per second], away from the earth and from a certain point allowed to return at the same speed, he would not become a second older even though the time of the earth had elapsed a thousand years while he was on his journey.[29]

Einstein's observations about the nature of time and space parallel verses in the Quran.

> *To God belongs the future of the heavens and the earth. As far as He is concerned, the end of the world (the Hour) is a blink of an eye away, or even closer. God is Omnipotent. (16:77)*

> *He said, "How long have you lasted on earth? How many years?"*
> *They said, "We lasted a day or part of a day. Ask those who counted."*
> *He said, "In fact, you stayed but a brief interim, if you only knew." (23:112-114)*

> *All matters are controlled by Him from the heaven to the earth. To Him, the day is equivalent to one thousand of your years. (32:5)*

Edison concluded that the chemical makeup of man reflects the existence of a Supreme Chemist. Einstein concluded that man's intellect emanates from a Supreme

Intelligence. Einstein contemplated something greater, and he experienced a "religious feeling" and "humble amazement." Unlike Einstein and Edison, some individuals who regard themselves as seekers of truth are unwilling to acknowledge that human beings are configured in a special way for a special purpose that transcends Einstein's infinitesimal "small patch" of physical reality.

Grunts Are Not Words

The expanse of man's verbal and cognitive abilities rules out the idea that man acquired such characteristics as a function of natural selection. Mature primates cannot remotely approach a child's reasoning and information processing ability.

Our discussion of recent efforts to teach language to chimpanzees makes it clear that a young chimp's linguistic progress is certainly not identical to that of a human child. A child's acquisition of language seems amazingly effortless, given the complexity of the task. In contrast, it takes years of careful training to provide a chimp with a vocabulary of something over a hundred words.[30]

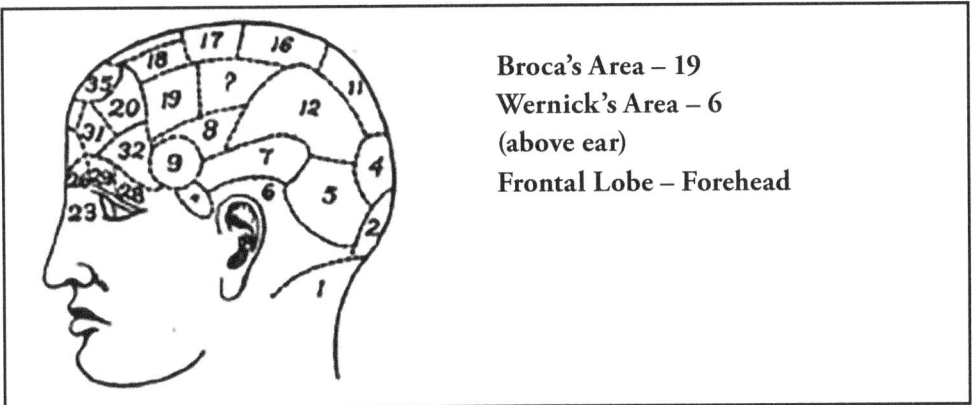

Broca's Area – 19
Wernick's Area – 6
(above ear)
Frontal Lobe – Forehead

Figure 1.2. Areas of Human Brain

Areas of the brain have been mapped according to their functions. Broca's Area is associated with speech, comprehension, and writing. In the temporal lobe, Wernick's Area is associated with understanding, speech, and language. A chimp's learned "vocabulary" is confined to physical gestures, grunts, and hand signs associated with simple, discrete actions. This elementary conditioning and imitation requires little higher-level functioning. In the human brain, the frontal lobe and cerebral cortex are associated with executive functions, control, organization, and planning. Broca's and Wernick's Areas play major roles in learning language, developing the ability to abstract, and making logical inferences. There are no equivalent areas in the ape brain. Thirty years ago, research exploring the linguistic capabilities of apes had all but closed the debate about whether apes can learn language and higher concepts.

> Can chimpanzees be said to use language in the human sense of the word? ... Psychologist Herbert Terrance, who spent four years teaching sign language to a young male chimp named Nim Chimpsky...became convinced that his chimp was indeed combining words into grammatical utterances comparable to a child's first sentences. But on analyzing all the data he collected, Terrance began to doubt that Nim's accomplishments were really as sophisticated as a human child's. For one thing, a child's sentences quickly grow in both length and complexity, incorporating correct rules of syntax. Nim did not progress in this way.... [M]any of the things [Nim] uttered were a partial imitation of something a teacher just said.... Terrance believes that chimps may have the *potential* to create grammatical sentences, but the ultimate evidence that they in fact do this has not yet been obtained.[31]

Research results obtained in the last four decades have not departed far from Dr. Terrance's conclusions. Hundreds of studies hypothesizing links between humans and apes have been conducted. Some studies have yielded information about similarities in limited discrete actions but no studies have provided *new information about human behavior.* Many post-nineteenth-century researchers are unaware that this line of inquiry was born out of a desire to deny the existence of God, buttress the ape-to-man evolution myth, and deny the fact that human beings are born in accord with God's laws in an ordered universe. Exclusive to humans, complex language production is entwined with the ability to read, conceptualize, understand symbols, and engage in higher-order executive functions. For some individuals, the thesis that apes can perform such operations reduces the bio-genetic "divide" between apes and humans, and keeps the belief alive that humans are *not* a special creation. However, in the Quran, the behavior of apes is described as "despicable."

You have known about those among you who desecrated the Sabbath. We said to them, "Be you as despicable as apes." (2:65)

When they continued to defy the commandments, we said to them, "Be you despicable apes." (7:166)

The parallel drawn in verses 2:65 and 7:166 between a chronic refusal to heed God's commands and the "despicable" behavior of apes is interesting. The analogy implies a regression from human reason and healthy behavior to base, contemptible, despicable, abhorrent (*khaase'een*) behavior.

Do not confound the truth with falsehood, nor shall you conceal the truth, knowingly. (2:42)

This is because you used to rejoice in false doctrines, on earth, and you used to promote them. (40:75)

Have they found gods on earth who can create? (21:21)

We have created you, if you could only believe! (56:57)

11

Toward The Soul And The Great Chain Of Being

After clarifying the interspecies evolution myth and its negative impact on the understanding of man's purpose, we proceed to a nonmaterial "something" in man upon which his nature and personality rest. That something is *the soul*. An individual who persists in clinging to the idea that he or she is solely derived from random, loosely knitted physical elements, suppresses his or her intuitive awareness of the soul. In contrast, individuals who embrace three *confirmed* truths understand that man is not a fortuitous life form in a purposeless universe. ….

First truth: creation is the outcome of a Source that conceptualizes, calculates, configures, designs, and constructs.
Second truth: the components of life did not create themselves.
Third truth: humans are spiritual beings enshrouded in physical forms in this world.

These truths constitute the foundation of the psychospiritual study of personality. This foundation is more clearly articulated in cultures that acknowledge the spiritual reality underlying physical existence.

In the tenth century C.E., a group of spiritually inspired Islamic scholars known as the Ikhwan Al-Safa gave the world the *Great Chain of Being,* their comprehensive treatise on the nature of creation.[32] Referring to people who believe that life and motion emanate exclusively from physical bodies, the Ikhwan al-Safa said:

They do not know that there is along with the body a substance which is ultimately spiritual and invisible. This is the Soul, which they describe as

16

being an accident, by means of which change occurs in the body. It is this, that is, the Soul, by which actions appear in bodies.[33]

The Ikhwan-al-Safa also said:

A particular entity has a position in the great chain of Being depending upon the degree to which it participates in Being and Intelligence…the degree to which anything possesses beauty, or, in other words, participates in the Absolute Beauty which is an inner attribute of God…. Man is the central link in the great chain; below him stands the animal kingdom, and above, the world of angels, and he is connected to one domain as well as the other.[34]

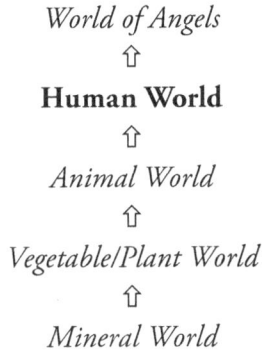

World of Angels
⇧
Human World
⇧
Animal World
⇧
Vegetable/Plant World
⇧
Mineral World

Figure 2.1. Great Chain of Being (simplified)

Reflecting the *gradation* of created worlds or spheres, the Great Chain of Being is based on *interior faculties* rather than anatomical physical features and external behavior. According to the Ikhwan and now noted by scientists, *it is the elephant, not the ape, that is closest to man.* Based on the degree it participates in Universal Being and Intelligence, the elephant ranks highest in intelligence in the animal world. Unlike apes, elephants exhibit complex thought processes, an ability to learn to associate alphabets and symbols with specific behaviors, a capacity to mourn, and they have an intricate social structure. In her article, *Elephant Intelligence*, Claire Bradon said,

Should elephants be moved to near the top of the animal-intelligence list? For the first time, remote-control cameras disguised as dung-heaps have infiltrated African elephant herds…. "The communication and understanding is so evident when you get inside the herd," says film-maker John Downer. "I know of no other species, apart from ourselves, who gather to greet a newborn and equally appear to mourn their dead relatives."… Self-awareness is another key ability of conscious beings. To be conscious is, first, to be conscious of yourself - to be aware that 'I' am a being separate from others and the world around 'me'. Just as a person looking into a mirror and seeing a dirty face will try to wipe it, it has been found that an elephant studying its reflection will try to rub smudges off its forehead with its trunk. Many behavioural researchers consider that ability to be a hallmark of complex intelligence…. Elephants are very adept at tool-use, which they learn from the older matriarchs…With evidence mounting of elephant intelligence, wide-ranging communication and apparent awareness of the feelings of their fellow group members, it must suggest a need for a rise in their status both on the intelligence spectrum and for protection against culling and poaching.[35]

Centuries before Charles Darwin presented his theory of evolution, the Ikhwan realized that positioning for survival and adaptation is prewired into every creature.

"Adaptation to the environment" is not the result of struggles for life or "survival of the fittest," but comes from the wisdom of the Creator.[36]

Each species is the *fittest* within its realm and specific roles. Extinct species were not pre-fitted to survive beyond their purpose in the grand scheme. For example, dinosaurs ate humongous amounts of plants (and some smaller animals). The terrain that they lived on contained sufficient foliage and vegetation for them to thrive. Lodged beneath the earth for millions of years, their carbonized remains are refined by man into fuel to light fires; oil to heat dwellings; gasoline to run motors and engines; asphalt for roads, solvents, rubber, latex, waxes, plastics, and many other products. Dinosaurs did not enter this world or leave it by happenstance. Like the DNA-shaped nebula in the cosmos and intracellular DNA, dinosaurs' presence and departure, and the factors that led to their departure were also by design. An All-Wise Supreme Being created and positioned each world of beings so that the final scheme satisfies all creatures' needs and serves the purpose of creation. Such was the case with the dinosaurs. Similar to intracellular operations, no external world on the cosmic Chain of Being is primitive or ancestral in relation to worlds that come after it. Encompassing the human, animal, plant, and mineral worlds, the final scheme should be regarded as a "perfect, balanced" ecological system.

> As minerals serve plants and plants animals, so do animals in turn serve man, who therefore comes to this world later than all of them, since each has come after the kingdom upon which it depends."…[P]rovidential wisdom stipulates that an animal be given no other organs than these. If it were otherwise, the animal would be hindered and its safety and continued existence endangered.[37]

Universe in the Quran

Some Quran chapter titles reflect the universe and worlds on the Chain of Being. When arranged based on the Chain, the titles are: *The Light, The Galaxies, The Stars, The Heights, The Sun, The Moon, The Dawn, The Forenoon, The Afternoon, The Night, The Thunder, The Dunes, The Iron, The Fig, The Spider, The Ant, The Bee, The Cow, The Livestock, The Elephant, The Gallopers, The Jinn, The Human, The Embryo,* and *The People.*

The Light (Al-Nur) is an attribute of God. In revealed scriptures, light is an allegory for Absolute Consciousness, the Source of all things, and Divine guidance.

> *God is the light of the heavens and the earth. The allegory of His light is that of a concave mirror behind a lamp that is placed inside a glass container. The glass container is like a bright, pearl-like star. The fuel thereof is supplied from a blessed oil-producing tree, that is neither eastern, nor western. Its oil is almost self-radiating; needs no fire to ignite it. Light upon light. God guides to His light whoever wills (to be guided). God thus cites the parables for the people. God is fully aware of all things. (24:35)*

God revealed that all matters pertinent to psychospiritual recovery and growth are in the Quran.

All the creatures on earth, and all the birds that fly with wings, are communities like you. We did not leave anything out of this book. To their Lord, all these creatures will be summoned. (6:38)

A closer look at the selected Quran chapter titles illustrates how the Quran encompasses the entire creation accessible to human consciousness. *The Galaxies* refers to the universes, cosmos, and worlds beyond this solar system. *The Stars, The Moon, The Dawn, The Forenoon,* and *The Night* refer to the star-laden universe; celestial, solar, and lunar lights; and the alternation of light and darkness on earth. *The Heights* refer to the regions between the highest universe and this terrestrial plane. *The Thunder* refers to the stunning powerful sound that accompanies lightning, the forces that cause it, and the forces that lead to rainfall and electric valences in the atmosphere and in the earth. *The Winds* flow along transoceanic currents and over continents, drive moisture-laden clouds, contribute to temperature change, and are part of the evaporation-precipitation system that recycles water so land animals, insects, and plants have water. *The Iron* and *The Dunes* refer to the elements and sand on the earth's surface. The wind carries the fine rock particles that compose sand to form sand dunes, sand pits, and sand bars over the earth's surface. In deserts, sand constitutes the surface land mass. A fact first revealed in the Quran (57:25), *Iron* was created amidst the tremendous heat and energy of the Big Bang—the cataclysmic explosion that lead to the formation of the cosmos—universes, galaxies, planets, and all elements, including the elements that constitute the human body.

... And we sent down the iron, wherein there is strength, and many benefits for the people. All this in order for God to distinguish those who would support Him and His messengers, on faith. God is Powerful, Almighty. (57:25, partial)

God was the Cause of the Big Bang, and His forces detonated the fuse. *The Fig* refers to fruits and the plant world. Figs are the fruit of palm trees, and palm trees rank highest in the plant world. *The Spider, The Ant, The Bee, The Cow, The Livestock, The Elephant,* and *The Gallopers* (that is, horses used as means of travel and for other uses) refer to the world of animals, including insects. *The Bee* ranks highest in the insect world. *The Elephant* ranks highest in the animal world. *The Jinn* refers to the descendents of Satan, spiritual creatures that are confined to this lowest universe, reside on earth, and are assigned to human beings. Evil jinn promote rebellion against God's guidance. *The Embryo* is the biological nest for prenatal life that culminates in the birth of a newborn. *The Human* and *The People* refer to the highest creature residing in this world. All worlds on earth were created for other creatures and to support and serve humans.

Terrestrial and Celestial Worlds

And He is the One who made the stars to guide you during the darkness, on land and on sea. We thus clarify the revelations for people who know. (6:97)

Do the unbelievers not realize that the heaven and the earth used to be one solid mass that we exploded into existence?[Big Bang] And from water we made all living things. Would they believe? (21:30)

We have adorned the lowest heaven with adorning planets. (37:6)

We created above you seven universes in layers, and we are never unaware of a single creature in them. (23:17)

Thus, He completed the seven universes in two days, and set up the laws for every universe. And we adorned the lowest universe with lamps, and placed guards around it. Such is the design of the Almighty, the Omniscient. (41:12)

He is the One who made the earth habitable for you, and created for you roads therein, that you may follow the right way. (43:10)

He created the earth for all creatures. (55:10)

He is the One who put the earth at your service. Roam its corners, and eat from His provisions. To Him is the final summoning. (67:15)

The World of Elements

He is the One who created the heavens and the earth in six days—and His (earthly) domain was completely covered with water—in order to test you, to distinguish those among you who work righteousness…. (11:7, partial)

He is the One who creates for you, from the green trees, fuel which you burn for light. (36:80)

…And from water we made all living things. Would they believe? (21:30, partial)

He is the One who merges the two seas; one is fresh and palatable, while the other is salty and undrinkable. And He separated them with a formidable, inviolable barrier (evaporation). (25:53)

… And we sent down the iron, wherein there is strength, and many benefits for the people. All this in order for God to distinguish those who would support Him and His messengers, on faith. God is Powerful, Almighty. (57:25, partial)

The World of Plants

He is the One who sends down from the sky water, whereby we produce all kinds of plants. We produce from the green material multitudes of complex grains, palm trees with hanging clusters, and gardens of grapes, olives and pomegranate; fruits that are similar, yet dissimilar. Note their fruits as they grow and ripen. These are signs for people who believe. (6:99)

He sends down from the sky water for your drink, and to grow trees for your benefit. (16:10)

And we created the earth, and scattered on it mountains, and grew in it all kinds of beautiful plants… And we sent from the sky blessed water, to grow with it gardens and grains to be harvested. (50:7, 9)

The World of Animals

The example of such disbelievers is that of parrots who repeat what they hear of sounds and calls, without understanding. Deaf, dumb, and blind; they cannot understand. (2:171)

They consult you concerning what is lawful for them; say, "Lawful for you are all good things, including what trained dogs and falcons catch for you...." (5:4, partial).

All fish of the sea are made lawful for you to eat.... You shall reverence God, before whom you will be summoned.... (5:96, partial)

Consequently, we sent upon them the flood, the locusts, the lice, the frogs, and the blood—profound signs. But they maintained their arrogance. They were evil people.... When they continued to defy the commandments, we said to them, "Be you despicable apes." (7:133, 166)

And (He created) the horses, the mules, and the donkeys for you to ride, and for luxury. Additionally, He creates what you do not know.... And in the livestock there is a lesson for you: we provide you with a drink from their bellies. From the midst of digested food and blood, you get pure milk, delicious for the drinkers... And your Lord inspired the bee: build homes in mountains and trees, and in (the hives) they build for you. Then eat from all the fruits, following the design of your Lord, precisely. From their bellies comes a drink of different colors, wherein there is healing for the people. This should be (sufficient) proof for people who reflect.... Do they not see the birds committed to fly in the atmosphere of the sky? None holds them up in the air except God. This should be (sufficient) proof for people who believe.(16:8, 66, 68-69, 79)

Eight kinds of livestock: regarding the two kinds of sheep, and the two kinds of goats.... (6:143, partial)

O people, here is a parable that you must ponder carefully: the idols you set up beside God can never create a fly, even if they banded together to do so. Furthermore, if the fly steals anything from them, they cannot recover it; weak is the pursuer and the pursued. (22:73)

We then inspired him: "Make the watercraft under our watchful eyes, and in accordance with our inspiration. When our command comes, and the atmosphere boils up, put on it a pair of every kind (of your domesticated animals).... (23:27, partial)

He then threw his staff, whereupon it became a profound snake. (26:32)

The allegory of those who accept other masters beside God is that of the spider and her home; the flimsiest of all homes is the home of the spider, if they only knew. (29:41)

Consequently, the fish [whale] swallowed him, and he was the one to blame. (37:142)

Among His proofs is the creation of the heavens and the earth, and the creatures He spreads in them. He is able to summon them, when He wills. (42:29)

He is the One who created all kinds, in pairs (male and female), and He created for you ships and livestock to ride. (43:12)

Also in your creation, and the creation of all the animals, there are proofs for people who are certain. (45:4)

He asked his family to prepare a fat calf. (51:26)

Running like zebras. Who are fleeing from the lion! (74:50-51)

By the fast gallopers [on horses]. Igniting sparks. (100:1-2)

Why do they not reflect on the camels and how they are created? (88:17)

Have you noted what your Lord did to the people of the elephant? (105:1)

The World of Humans

O people, observe your Lord; the One who created you from one being, and created from it its mate, then spread from the two many men and women. You shall regard God, by whom you swear, and regard the parents. God is watching over you. (4:1)

Your Lord said to the angels, "I am creating a human being from aged mud, like the potter's clay." (15:28)

O people, if you have any doubt about resurrection, (remember that) we created you from dust, and subsequently from a tiny drop, which turns into a hanging (embryo), then it becomes a fetus that is given life or deemed lifeless. We thus clarify things for you. We settle in the wombs whatever we will for a predetermined period. We then bring you out as infants, then you reach maturity. While some of you die young, others live to the worst age, only to find out that no more knowledge can be attained beyond a certain limit. Also, you look at a land that is dead, then as soon as we shower it with water, it vibrates with life and grows all kinds of beautiful plants. (22:5)

He is the One who created from water a human being, then made him reproduce through marriage and mating. Your Lord is Omnipotent. (25:54)

He is the One who perfected everything He created, and started the creation of the human from clay…. He shaped him and blew into him from His spirit. And He gave you the hearing, the eyesight, and the brains; rarely are you thankful. (32:7, 9)

"Once I design him, and blow into him from My spirit, you shall fall prostrate before him." (38:72)

Creator of the human beings. He taught them how to distinguish. (55:3-4)

I did not create the jinns and the humans except to worship Me alone. (51:56)

We created the human from a liquid mixture, from two parents, in order to test him. Thus, we made him a hearer and a seer. (76:2)

The World of Angels

Recall that your Lord said to the angels, "I am placing a representative (a temporary god) on Earth." They said, "Will You place therein one who will spread evil therein and shed blood, while we sing Your praises, glorify You, and uphold Your absolute authority?" He said, "I know what you do not know." (2:30)

Shifts (of angels) take turns, staying with each one of you—they are in front of you and behind you. They stay with you, and guard you in accordance with God's commands. (13:11, partial)

He sends down the angels with the revelations, carrying His commands, to whomever He chooses from among His servants: "You shall preach that there is no other god beside Me; You shall reverence Me." (16:2)

To God prostrates everything in the heavens and everything on earth—every creature—and so do the angels; without the least arrogance. (16:49)

Recall that we said to the angels, "Fall prostrate before Adam." They fell prostrate, except Satan; he refused. (20:116)

Say, "You will be put to death by the angel in whose charge you are placed, then to your Lord you will be returned." (32:11)

He is the One who helps you, together with His angels, to lead you out of darkness into the light. He is Most Merciful towards the believers. (33:43)

Those who proclaim: "Our Lord is God," then lead a righteous life, the angels descend upon them: "You shall have no fear, nor shall you grieve. Rejoice in the good news that Paradise has been reserved for you." (41:30)

The heavens above them almost shatter, out of reverence for Him, and the angels praise and glorify their Lord, and they ask forgiveness for those on earth. Absolutely, God is the Forgiver, Most Merciful. (42:5)

Two recording (angels), at right and at left, are constantly recording. (50:17)

Some individuals ask, "Where do I fit in this scheme of things or all these worlds?" The answer first lies in the innate human awareness of a Supreme Being and in revealed scripture. Humans have higher consciousness and can question why they exist and seek the Ultimate Reality. In the Quran, the answer is provided in the context of the development of the soul (i.e., the true self). The worlds in this life provide a human habitat with life-sustaining provisions. All worlds are described in the Quran as united and in submission to God. Human beings along with wayward jinn are the only exceptions. The worlds are permeated with information (signs) that beacon individuals back to the reverence of God.

Sustained personality development starts when a person acknowledges his or her spiritual nature and purpose, and proceeds to fulfill that purpose. The Quran makes it clear that the human being is part of the Great Chain of Being. Individual psychospiritual personality development occurs when a person heeds information about the worlds in creation, recognizes that there is much more to life than satisfying fleeting sensory urges, and seeks the "much more." The path to self-knowledge is not a lifetime-long "coming out party" merely for an individual to distinguish himself or herself from others.

> In the universe, where the wisdom of the Creator is to be seen everywhere, every occurrence has its reason and shows the wisdom of God, so that each creature possesses those faculties which conform to its needs…. "Thy soul, oh Brother, is one of the pure forms. Use your efforts then to know it. Thou willst succeed probably in saving it from the ocean of matter to raise it from the abyss of the body and deliver it from the prison of Nature."[38]

Each human soul is a pure form. Housed in a physical body, the soul is "the spiritual faculty in man…the original spirit in man first created by God."[39] *The original spirit is the true self, the pure form, the true personality.* The true personality should be properly nurtured, so the soul-person can learn where he or she fits in the scheme of things, recovery from psychospiritual illness and be restored to his or her nature of innate submission to God. At some point, each person's life in this world will end. At another point, this cosmos will cease to exist. Each person will be ranked according to his or her psychospiritual development (i.e., how close the person comes to Absolute Beauty and Light). Each individual has what he or she needs for his or her soul to flourish, by feeding the yearning to return to the Lord of all worlds. Each person is preparing to ascend or descend, to draw near or fall away, to eternally rejoice or eternally regret, to enter the domain of Absolute Light, Beauty, and Bliss (the Presence of God) or enter the domain of Darkness, Horror, and Despair.

> *The One who created death and life for the purpose of distinguishing those among you who would do better. He is the Almighty, the Forgiving. (67:2)*

999

Personality Universals

The DNA genetic "blueprint" of life;, and the clear "footprints" of intelligence, order, and design on a celestial, terrestrial, and human level; and complementary Quran verses provide the correct approach to the study of personality. Eternal and unchanging, the correct approach acknowledges the presence of intelligence, purpose, order, design, and meaning throughout creation. The approach also acknowledges the overriding influence of a Spiritual Absolute, a Divine Being who created and fashioned all worlds. Each person is invested with universally shared psychospiritual attributes. When properly cultivated, each person's attributes give rise to a personality in submission to his or her Creator. Distinct characteristics that make an individual unique from others are the common threads in definitions of personality. Psychospiritual approaches to the study of personality highlight factors that contribute to individual spiritual character formation. Relative causes of personality are as numerous as the multifaceted nature of human experience.

It is incorrect to speak of non-human species as having personality. Using language applicable to humans, individuals describe animal behavior in human terms and attribute human emotions to animals. To an extent, human perceptions and observations about some animal behavior are correct. Yet, we often project human emotions onto animals. Animal species are in communities designed for their natures and purpose in the broader scheme. Animals are souls that repented to God while in His Presence after doubting His Absolute Power and Authority. God forgave them. Like us, animals live in this dimension for a while. Unlike us, they instinctively submit to God. Animals do not have a false self that rebels against the Creator. The souls invested in animals return to Paradise.

All the creatures on earth, and all the birds that fly with wings, are communities like you. We did not leave anything out of this book. To their Lord, all these creatures will be summoned. (6:38)

Also in your creation, and the creation of all the animals, there are proofs for people who are certain. (45:4)

A person might decry, "This is ridiculous. How could you verify such a thing?" Even though some animals may share the same terrain or waters, animals live in distinct communities (6:38). Each species-specific community of creatures receives Divine guidance. In the case of animals, there guidance is reflected in their instinctive behavior. No one can question animals about their communities, their abdication of free will, and their awareness of a Divine Being. This knowledge is not amenable to *direct* scientific verification, if verification necessitates using observable measurable methods. The Creator placed a miraculous verifiable mathematical Code in the Quran so that open-minded individuals could be certain about such matters. Man is surrounded by creatures that submit to the Creator.

It is important to know what *inner* characteristics distinguish humankind from other species. The inner characteristics cannot be understood or explained solely in the languages of physical and biological sciences. The *psychospiritual* character of human personality has no parallel in the animal kingdom.

The Human Being: A Special Creation

The distinctive characteristic of the human being is a link to the Divine Spirit. The inner self can only be properly understood in this context. Constituting a distinct species, humans did not evolve from a lower life form. *Intra-species evolution is a fact. Interspecies evolution is not a fact, nor is it possible.* Life on earth began in water, and no organism can exist without it. However, earthly life's origin in water does not mean that man evolved from the first water inundated proteins and microorganisms, then eventually into apes, and finally into human beings.

O people, observe your Lord; the One who created you from one being, and created from it its mate, then spread from the two many men and women. You shall regard God, by whom you swear, and regard the parents. God is watching over you. (4:1)

He is the One who created you from mud, then predetermined your life span, a life span that is known only to Him. Yet, you continue to doubt. (6:2)

Your Lord said to the angels, "I am creating a human being from aged mud, like the potter's clay. Once I perfect him, and blow into him from My Spirit (Ruhi), you shall fall prostrate before him." (15:28-29)

He is the One who perfected everything He created, and started the creation of the human from clay. (32:7)

He is the One who created the two kinds, male and female—from a tiny drop of semen. (53:45-46)

Verse 4:1 alludes to the processes of human creation and procreation. The phrases "dust," "clay," "aged mud," and "certain kind of mud" (3:59, 15:28, 23:12, and 32:7) suggest that man's physical form was configured in *a special way* to be uniquely fitted for human activity. An external designer infused specific elements (referred to as dust) and fashioned every aspect of the human (*ih'san*) physical form.[40] The human body was configured so that when humans interact with the physical world, they acquire information about this terrestrial realm and aspects of the celestial world. By virtue of the nature of the human nervous system and sensory apparatus, humans can harness some natural forces, and discover the nature and origins of things, including themselves. In the context of personality development, the information that a person derives from proper use of his or her biological 'equipment' enables the person to arrive at the understanding that the world, including the self, is the handiwork of a higher being.

Verses 53:45-46 reveal that the contents of a father's seminal fluid determine a baby's gender. The phrase, "from a tiny drop of semen," rules out the possibility that a human composed verse 53:46. In Arabic, the word for "tiny drop" (*noot'fa*) is equivalent to a microscopic portion. In this case, it refers to a microscopic portion of semen. In the age that the Quran was revealed, man had no awareness of the microscopic world. A functional microscope was invented in the sixteenth century, approximately 830 years after the revelation of the Quran.

We created the human being from a certain kind of mud. (23:12)

O people, if you have any doubt about resurrection, (remember that) we created you from dust, and subsequently from a tiny drop, which turns into a hanging (embryo), then it becomes a fetus that is given life or deemed lifeless. We thus clarify things for you. We settle in the wombs whatever we will for a predetermined period. We then bring you out as infants, then you reach maturity. While some of you die young, others live to the worst age, only to find out that no more knowledge can be attained beyond a certain limit. Also, you look at a land that is dead, then as soon as we shower it with water, it vibrates with life and grows all kinds of beautiful plants. (22:5)

Verse 22:5 says that a land that is dead "vibrates with life" after contact with water. No physical life can exist without water. At first glance, a person does not see soil "vibrate" other than in the movement of particles during rainfall. Scientists determined that in a fertile section of the earth in an area one meter in diameter, there are thirty million bacteria.[41] After rainfall, particles in the soil are ionized. In the second stage, the particles swell. In the third stage, the fertilization process starts with the germination of seeds.[42] Likewise, a similar process occurs when conception takes place in the womb. This is another example of a process that occurs in the microcosm (human body) and macrocosm (in this case, the earth).

Each human cell contains twenty-three pairs of chromosomes. Human DNA is approximately an average of 6 feet, 6 inches in total length. (6 + 6 = 12).[43] The correspondence between the chapter and verse number (23:12) and the facts that there are twenty-three pairs of human chromosomes, and human DNA is an average of 6 feet 6 inches (12) is not a coincidence. *It is possible that the Creator numerically coded verse 23:12 to reflect the human DNA molecular structure.* This structure underlies the phrase, *"a certain kind of mud."* Barren sterile soil does not contain building blocks of organic life, let alone the genetic "blueprint" for a human being. Verse 23:12 points to a Creator who instructed angelic forces in how to fashion the human form. The phrase, *"We created,"* refers to angels' participation in the human creation process.

The human body consists of twenty-five essential elements (Table 2:1). Imagine placing the twenty-five elements in a huge flask. Over millions of years and supposedly on their own, fixed amounts of the elements morph into different life forms, coalesce into an ape, and finally a human being. The operation of an Intelligent Being is the only logical explanation of how the precise mix of these twenty-five elements could become a human body. The fifty-seventh chapter of the Quran is titled "Iron" ("Hadeed") and the element is mentioned in verse 57:25. The geametrical value of the word "Hadeed" is 57 (19 x 3). The sum of the atomic numbers (weights)[44] of the other 24 elements in the human body is 577 (5+7+7 = 19). Iron was created in a higher universe amidst the Big Bang and "sent down" to this universe. Iron is a major element in the earth's core, and iron binds to proteins in the center of human cells. Besides being an essential element in all life forms, including the human body, iron plays a major role in the formation of the earth's electromagnetic field. Iron is the strongest and most stable element on earth.

… And we sent down the iron, wherein there is strength and many benefits for the people… (57:25, partial)

When verses 23:12 and 57:25 are written as two numbers (i.e., 2,312 and 5,725), the sum is 8,037 (19 x 423). You may conclude that the sum of these specific verses is no different from the sum of any two Quran verses that equals a multiple of 19.[45] *However, each chapter and verse number in these two verses is specifically related to human creation and the human micro-biological structure.* There are twenty-three pairs of human chromosomes; the estimated length of a DNA molecule in a human cell is up to twelve centimeters; there are twenty-five essential elements in the human body, and the element iron (Hadeed) plays a significant role. Without iron, cells could not receive energy and oxygen via the blood.

Table 3.1 The Twenty-Five Essential Elements in the Human Body

Element (Atomic #)	Found in/Purpose:	Rank/Amount in Body
H Hydrogen (1)	Living plants	Oxygen
C Carbon (6)	Sun, stars, comets, planets, meteorites	Carbon
N Nitrogen (7)	Living plants	Hydrogen
O Oxygen (8)	Organic compounds, living plants; most abundant element in the sun	Nitrogen
F Fluorine (9)	Electronegative gas	Calcium
Na Sodium (11)	Sun, stars, animal nutrition; fourth most abundant element on earth	Phosphorus
Mg Magnesium (12)	Brines, wells, sea water, earth's crust, plant and animal life	Sulphur
Si Silicon (14)	Sun, stars, earth's crust, meteorites.	Potassium
P Phosphorus (15)	Cell protoplasm, nervous tissue, bones	Sodium
S Sulphur (16)	Meteorites, fats, body fluids, skeletal materials	Chlorine
Cl Chlorine (17)	Found with sodium	Magnesium
K Potassium (19)	Plants	Silicon
Ca Calcium (20)	Leaves, bones, teeth, shells	Iron
V Vanadium (23)	Minerals, rock, iron ores	Fluorine
Cr Chromium (24)	Ore deposits	Zinc
Mn Manganese (25)	Floor of oceans, depolarizer of cells.	Copper
Fe Iron (26)	Sun, stars, earth's crust	Manganese
Co Cobalt (27)	Minerals, meteorites	Tin
Ni Nickel (28)	Meteorites	Iodine
Cu Copper (29)	Minerals	Selenium
Zn Zinc (30)	An ore, essential for human and animal growth	Nickel
Se Selenium (34)	Electric conductor, essential trace element	Molybdenun
Mo Molybdenun(42)	Minerals, plants, metabolic processes	Vanadium
Sn Tin (50)	Earth deposits	Chromium
I Iodine (53)	Sea water, seaweed, cell regeneration.	Cobalt

It is a stretch of logic to conclude that such intricate sophisticated operations (e.g., the balance and equilibrium of disparate elements in the human body, procreation and gender determination, the DNA/chromosomal blueprint, and mechanisms for "feeding" oxygen and energy to cells) are chance occurrences.

The similarity between the creation of Jesus and Adam is confirmed mathematically. Both names are mentioned in the Quran twenty-five times. By God's command ("Be"), Jesus was conceived in the womb of his mother. His gender identity did not depend on the *importation* of a Y chromosome from semen. Yet, Jesus' physical body consisted of the same essential twenty-five elements and chromosome/DNA structure as any human male. God and His angels sent "our Spirit" in the *form* of a human being who, in turn, initiated the conception of life in Mary's womb. The Creator has no need of anyone, anything, or a condition to bring a life into being (verse 3:59). Adam and Eve did not have parents, and Jesus had no father. Parents are *not* the irreducible complex structures from whence human life emerges.

The example of Jesus, as far as God is concerned, is the same as that of Adam; He created him from dust, then said to him, "Be," and he was. (3:59)

In verse 3:59, the word *dust* refers to minute particles or elements. The Creator's commands "Be," and brings whatever He wills into existence. All physical life forms are created from microscopic mixtures of elements. While there is no time in the presence of God, in this spatial-temporal dimension, such processes "take time." Some creatures' entire life spans are less than several minutes of the human experience of time.[46] God creates the conditions and elements of life.

We created the human from a liquid mixture, from two parents, in order to test him. Thus, we made him a hearer and a seer. (76:2)

While a barrier separated her from them, we sent to her our Spirit. He went to her in the form of a human being. She said, "I seek refuge in the Most Gracious, that you may be righteous." He said, "I am the messenger of your Lord, to grant you a pure son." She said, "How can I have a son, when no man has touched me; I have never been unchaste." He said, "Thus said your Lord, 'It is easy for Me. We will render him a sign for the people and mercy from us. This is a predestined matter.'" (19:17-21)

The Spiritually Disguised Personality

In the early nineteenth century, a group of scientists and intellectuals in the West promoted a concept of freedom void of moral responsibility and accountability. In his volume, *You Shall Be A Blessing*, the humanistic psychiatrist Dr. Alexander Muller elaborated on the social dialectic underpinning the ape-to-man thesis. Referencing the economic historian, Dr. Werner Sombart, Muller said:

> Werner Sombart really finds it surprising how eagerly people have read and accepted the theories about man's descent from the ape. Is there a reason to take such pleasure and pride in the theory that we descended from apes? According to Sombart's opinion, the explanation for this phenomenon is the desire for freedom in the nineteenth century. If a God existed, man would not be completely free or independent anymore. However, if the higher creatures originated from the lower ones, there really could be no God. The theories about the descent of man made God superfluous.[47]

Muller commented on the emergence of personality theories bereft of factors that researchers could not observe and quantify. Spiritual qualities of the human personality were dismissed as without foundation.

> He who seeks shall find. Werner Sombart calls the nineteenth century "the dark century in which we have forgotten everything that people knew for centuries." In reality, the epoch understood man less and less, but could explain him and all his behavior. In the hands of the researchers, man himself, his personality, disappeared at the same time. The nineteenth century was *the century of the "disguised personality"* (Fritz Kunkel). At the same time, the number of theories increased which tried to explain human behavior on a strictly scientific basis. These theories succeeded according to the researcher's own opinions.[48] (italics added)

Dr. Fritz Kunkel's "disguised personality" refers to the abandonment of perennial truths about the nature of human consciousness and psychological health for a "freedom" from accountability to a higher authority. The "disguised personality" hoists an irreligious ego as the real self and deletes the creative center of man—the psychospiritual connection to the Creator. Dr. Kunkel determined that nineteenth century man is "in the midst of a great psychological mutation." He said:

One must be ever-vigilant, knowing that which appears as selfless intent may be personality desire cleverly disguised. In short, the personality wants to believe itself to be the soul rather than an instrument of the soul. This it does through an act of self-deception by masquerading itself as the soul.... The distinction between the prompting of the soul and the spiritually disguised personality can be quite difficult. One's ability to make this distinction is enhanced when s/he remembers that personality motivations are always self-referencing at their core. Complete discernment of soul intention from personality pretense is the goal all disciples are working toward, and is a measure of placement upon the Path. It is our creative center, the Self, it is our positive relationship to God.[49]

Regarded as the father of western experimental psychology, the Marxist psychologist Dr. Wilhelm Wundt sought to divest psychology of spirit and free will. Wanting psychology to be accepted as a "hard" science, he believed that humans could be conditioned like animals in a laboratory. In their article entitled, "Death of the Soul," Mark Barber and Robert Daniels wrote:

Prior to Wundt, psychology had studied the human psyche or soul. But Wundt considered it to be a "useless waste of energy" to pursue something that he believed couldn't be observed or measured.... He purged all spiritual aspects from psychology and concentrated on the physical, intending, in his words, to "mark out a new domain of science."...For Wundt, man was merely an animal, a thing to be conditioned and controlled.... People lack self-determinism, Wundt claimed; they simply react to environmental stimuli. He felt that neither men, women nor children were capable of free will or volitional control... .[50]

The eminent social psychologist and humanistic philosopher, Dr. Eric Fromm, noted that in the nineteenth century a new freedom heralded in a "dead man" bereft of his spiritual center.

In the nineteenth century the problem was that God is dead; in the twentieth century the problem is that man is dead.[51]

In the shadow of the powerful privileged classes and the masses' political and economic servility, the European struggle for freedom during the eighteenth and nineteenth centuries demanded an "absolute freedom." No natural or social science, philosophy, or social movement was exempt from this mandate. Referring to the mandate, Muller commented:

> This freedom lead to individualism and maximum individual freedom, and developed so strongly toward ambition for power that man not only refused to accept an *outside* power, he also refused to accept a *higher* power. This is one of the deepest psychological causes of European atheism. In striving towards absolute freedom, one did not tolerate anything that could end freedom. It is as if a man said, "As long as there is something above me, I am not free; thus, there can be no God." …Nietzsche said, "If there were gods, how could I tolerate that I am not a god?" …Anything that proved the existence of God, one does not see because one did not want to see.[52]

Author of *The Science of Religion*, Yogi Paramahansa Yogananda, echoed the perennial truth dismissed by proponents of the new freedom and the "great psychological mutation." In 1924, Yogi Paramahansa Yogananda wrote:

> In the teachings of all religions, whether it be Christianity, Mohammedanism, or Hinduism, one truth is stressed: Until man knows himself as Spirit—the foundation of Bliss—he is limited by mortal concepts and subject to the inexorable laws of nature. Knowledge of his true being brings him eternal freedom.[53]

Once deemed their friend, science is bursting some skeptics' "bubble of hope" that a Supreme Designer or Creator is not necessary to explain existence. Invested with an ability to probe his inner nature, man was also granted knowledge of the world, in order to arrive at the awareness that the human is much more than this world.

> [T]he soul through this knowledge of cosmic realities can come to know itself better and be able to ultimately escape from the earthly prison into which it has fallen.[54]

In his book, *The Four Cardinal Virtues*, Dr. Josef Pieper translated an essay written by the philosopher Thomas Aquinas, clearly stating that personality is a unique human spiritual attribute. Quoting Aquinas, Dr. Pieper wrote:

Man, however, is a person—a spiritual being, a whole unto himself, a being that exists for itself and of itself, that wills its own proper perfection…. Indeed, man's personality, "the constitution of his spiritual being by virtue of which he is master of his own actions," even requires (requirit) says Thomas, that the Divine Providence guide the personality "for its own sake."…[T]he concept of the personality is set forth in all its elements: its freedom, imperishability, and responsibility for the whole of the world. If, on the contrary, man's personality is not acknowledged to be something wholly and entirely real, then right and justice cannot possibly be established.[55]

Original Human Nature

We are born in a state of obedience and submission to God. Referred to as Oneness or monotheism, the state constitutes the original human nature. The original human nature does not accommodate any form of polytheism. On the other hand, man has the ability to deviate from his inborn psychospiritual nature and has done so. The uprightness or the inner light placed in the original human nature (*fit'ra -al-insan*)[56] is an inclination to what is good, that is, a desire to please God and obey His Commands. While born in his true nature, man is weak. Individuals may choose to follow excessive prompts of a non-spiritual indulgent self (*nafs al-ammarah*) that, when unregulated, is prone to evil. The law-abiding self (*nafs al-lawwamah*) is a component of the original human nature. Dr. Carl Jung recognized that the spiritual conscience plays an important role in personality development. Dr. Jung wrote,

> Conscience, and particularly bad conscience, can be a gift from Heaven, a genuine grace, if used as a superior self-criticism. Self-criticism, as an introspective, discriminating activity, is indispensable to any attempt to understand one's own psychology.[57]

Dr. Jung described man as *homo religious*, that is, "the man who takes into account and carefully observes factors which influence him and through him, his general condition."

In personality, there is design, purpose, and planning that transcend this physical material scheme. Personality is teleological[58] in its works, its nature, and the ultimate destiny that it seeks to attain.

Therefore, you shall devote yourself to the religion of strict monotheism. Such is the natural instinct placed into the people by God. Such creation of God will never change. This is the perfect religion, but most people do not know. (30:30)

He created the heavens and the earth for a specific purpose, designed you and perfected your design, then to Him is the final destiny. (64:3)

We created man in the best design. Then turned him into the lowliest of the lowly. Except those who believe and lead a righteous life; they receive a reward that is well deserved. (95:4-6)

The destiny that personality naturally tends toward is to know what its origin is. We are spiritual salmon making our way upstream in the waters of physical life. Unlike real salmon, many people forget the purpose of the human journey. Regardless of doctrinal identification, anyone who transcends veils of satisfaction with less than truth realizes that human beings have a lofty spiritual nature. In October 1956, Pope Pius XII said,

This Divine origin of the human being is not simply an event which took place millennia ago; it is a present fact, a constant reality, because it is God who is constantly giving life to each human being, who makes him aware of His presence, who places in his heart an invincible attraction to the good, toward the absolute, toward perfect beatitude. The meaning of life can be summed up in a phrase, "the search for God," the search for Him who constantly calls His creatures to Him so that He can increasingly heap upon them the benefits of the fullness of His life and love.[59]

Common Sense and Limited Free Will

Each individual is created with a limited free will that the person may use to his or her advantage or detriment. To the extent that an individual's volitional acts are consistent with God's guidance, the person makes psychospiritual progress. When a person *intentionally* deviates from Divine guidance and psychospiritual design, the person retards his or her inner growth. Each individual has the freedom to mature into a healthy psychospiritual personality or an unhealthy one.

Each of you chooses the direction to follow; you shall race towards righteousness. Wherever you may be, God will summon you all. God is Omnipotent. (2:148)

We have offered the responsibility (freedom of choice) to the heavens and the earth, and the mountains, but they refused to bear it, and were afraid of it. But the human being accepted it; he was transgressing, ignorant. (33:72)

The common or *central sense* (*hiss mush'tarik*) is an inherent ability[60] to *perceive, distinguish, and combine* sensory input into conscious awareness. A God-given ability, the central sense enables a person to understand and be aware of subjective and objective reality. A creature cannot exercise limited free will and be accountable for its decisions and behavior if the creature is unaware of its own consciousness and life sphere. The central sense is unique to humans and gives each person the ability to reflect upon his or her consciousness.

The central sense is not the composite of other senses. If we use the computer as an analogy to discuss the human mind, other senses are the software programs loaded onto the computer. The central sense is like a computer's operating system (e.g., DOS or Windows). An operating system organizes, configures, and integrates the software programs in a manner that enables you to use the computer and the programs. Without an operating system, you cannot load programs into a computer. An operating system is greater than the software programs and the computer. A computer is only fully functioning when it runs off an *optimal* operating system. Some programs are faulty, and no computer is perfect. Likewise, no individual is perfect and without faults. The innate human operating system, however, is faultless.

The popular definition of the central sense as a *common* sense is inaccurate. The definition erroneously conveys the idea that good judgment automatically proceeds from having common sense. The "common" in common sense merely means that the ability is a *shared universal trait*. Most people assume that if a person has common sense, the person almost always uses it to reason and make good judgments. The reality of human fallibility dictates otherwise. Reason (*rashad*) is the *ability* to discern the correct course of action in a situation, independent of conflicting expectations and standards. Limited free will, the central sense, and reason are psychospiritual faculties. *Psychospiritual* faculties did not and cannot emerge from physical life forms.

God brought you out of your mothers' bellies knowing nothing, and He gave you the hearing, the eyesight, and the brains, that you may be appreciative. (16:78)

With the exception of reflex actions, most human behavior is functionally autonomous or free of the precipitating conditions that led to its emergence.[61] We retain conscious control over most of our actions. We can also modify the conditions wherein certain behaviors take place. In most situations, an individual has a choice between alternative courses of action, even if one option is no action. Personality and behavior are not solely determined by forces and influences beyond an individual's control. A frequent practice among some lawyers is to plead that individuals accused of serious violent crimes behaved "under duress," were "temporarily insane," are "victims of a turbulent past," or were "in a fit of passion or rage." The underlying implication is that the accused had no self-control when committing the act. In many cases, it is more accurate to conclude that the accused did not *choose or intend* to contain malevolent urges. Each person is responsible for his or her willful actions, including succumbing to malevolent urges.

An individual's life conditions often mirror the person's inner qualities. This principle also applies to a group that has the capacity to change its conditions as humans do. The prudent exercise of limited free will is essential to healthy personality development. Instead than passively wait for something to happen, a mature individual takes the initiative to modify his or her values, behavior, and outer conditions in order to foster psychospiritual growth.

Shifts (of angels) take turns, staying with each one of you—they are in front of you and behind you. They stay with you, and guard you in accordance with God's commands. Thus, God does not change the condition of any people unless they themselves [an'fufihim] make the decision to change. If God wills any hardship for any people, no force can stop it. For they have none beside Him as Lord and Master. (13:11)

Sheik Jaafar Idris aptly summarized the relationship between the will of God and human freedom:

Man cannot do anything against the will of God, but God has willed to give him the freedom to choose and the power to realize some of his intentions even if they go against the Guidance of God. One of the important areas in which God gave man to act is his internal state. But since much of what happens to man depends upon what kind of internal state he has, man can be said to be largely responsible for his own destiny.[62]

Souls that rebel against the Lord of the universe are allowed to pursue their chosen course. Were God to interfere with an individual's choice, the person would not have a limited free will. Incongruent with free will, no individual can be forced to believe in God.

Say, "Look at all the signs in the heavens and the earth." All the proofs and all the warnings can never help people who decided to disbelieve. (10:101)

Nothing happens to you except in accordance with God's will. Anyone who believes in God, He will guide his heart. God is fully aware of all things. (64:11)

Whatever you will is in accordance with God's will. God is Omniscient, Wise. (76:30)

Whatever you will is in accordance with the will of God, Lord of the universe. (81:29)

Higher Faculties and Moral Conscience

Man's higher faculties enable him to gain knowledge, exercise his limited free will, fashion human civilization, and distinguish between right and wrong. Intelligence includes the faculty of apprehension (*aql*), the capacity to apprehend or perceive the *meaning* of what enters awareness. Animals cannot perceive meaning. Human intelligence and the capacity for symbolic speech and language enable individuals to share their thoughts and discoveries with their contemporaries and future generations. The faculty of insight enables man to be aware of his physical, mental, and spiritual condition. Insight and intelligence are coupled with moral and spiritual self-surveillance, i.e., the law-abiding self (*an-nafs al-lawwamah*). The law-abiding self is like an inner counselor who enjoins righteousness and warns against evil.

Higher faculties in man point to a higher purpose and destiny, provided man *chooses to aspire* towards the higher purpose and destiny. Because human knowledge is incomplete and limited, man should rely on Divine guidance in understanding the meaning of self-development. If an individual foolishly ignores Divine guidance, he or she starts to regress to the lowest of states. In the context of psychospiritual development, intelligence is more than an ability to memorize and retain information and to engage in analytical reasoning. Regardless of his or her proficiency in calculation and reasoning, a person who ignores his or her conscience is not intelligent.

> *He bestows wisdom upon whomever He chooses, and whoever attains wisdom, has attained a great bounty. Only those who possess intelligence will take heed.* (2:269)

> *They are the ones who examine all words, then follow the best. These are the ones whom God has guided; these are the ones who possess intelligence.* (39:18)

Imagination and Intuition

The imagination (*quwwat al-khayaliyya*) is more than a mental ability to generate an inner screen to project new ideas, fantasies, and novel forms. Via the imagination, a person conceives of possibilities independent of the limits of external reality. For example, an individual can imagine himself or herself flying or, as the saying goes, "pigs flying." A person can imagine completing a task, and an artist can imagine how a painting will look prior to completing it. By means of the imagination, humans can transcend immediate parameters of time, place, and the known.

The imaginative faculty enables a person to hold a thought in consciousness. Constructive thoughts are building blocks for psychospiritual development. Destructive and deceptive thoughts lead to mental wandering and spiritual loss. The most prominent thought in a person's mind or imagination influences the person's perceptions and actions. The prominent thought in a person's imagination is like the tonal key that a musical instrument is tuned to. Although the musical notes are different, they are all related to each other by virtue of being in the same key. In the realm of human action, outer behaviors vary but a person's psychospiritual state is colored by spiritually constructive or destructive thoughts. The person who remembers (*dhikr*) God is protected from evil mentation[63] that besets the uncontrolled hedonistic imagination. The level of a person's *psychospiritual* consciousness depends on the growth of the person's real self. If a person is God-conscious, the person's spiritual "eye" is sharpened and focused to receive a diffusion of spiritual light. The guided use of the imaginative and intellectual faculties results in inner growth and a balanced personality. Chronic rejection of psychospiritual yearning warps the imagination. When extreme, the rejection leads to bizarre thoughts and behavior.

> *"I [Satan] will mislead them, I will entice them, I will command them to (forbid the eating of certain meats by) marking the ears of livestock, and I will command them to distort the creation of God." Anyone who accepts the devil as a lord, instead of God, has incurred a profound loss. (4:119)*

An attribute beyond exact definition, intuition includes an inner capacity or ability to know, independent of physical senses and conscious thought. The common adage, "I have a gut feeling," usually means a person's select awareness emanates from their innermost center, a non-physical center. Intuition taps into realities not immediately accessible through the senses. Intuition projects onto the mind what has *not* been derived through exertion or from experience. For example, human awareness of a Supreme Being is both intuitive and rational, the latter being a process of deduction. The rational mind depends on information derived from sensory input. Based on that information, an individual deduces certain facts, makes inferences, and draws certain conclusions. On the other hand, what a person intuitively gathers does not require external verification. Information that is intuitively gleaned is instantly experienced as real, despite a person's possible tendencies to later cast misgivings about it. To the extent that a person attempts to suppress his or her psychospiritual self, spiritual intuition is blunted.

Each Individual: Recognizable and Distinct

Each person has qualities and attributes that distinguish him or her from others. One sign of the uniqueness of each person is the fingerprint. Despite billions of people now alive and those who have departed from this world, no person's fingerprint is shared with another person. Even monozygotic twins do not have the same fingerprint. God reveals that He will reassemble our physical forms down to the minutest intricate detail. An individual's fingerprint pattern also reflects a unique constellation of genotypic characteristics.

Does the human being think that we will not reconstruct his bones? Yes indeed; we are able to reconstruct his fingertip. (75:3-4)

Seyyed Hossein Nasr observed that:

The uniqueness of the temperament of each individual indicates that each microcosm is a world of its own, not identical with any other microcosm. Yet, the repetition of the same basic humors in each constitution bears out the fact that each microcosm presents a morphological resemblance to other microcosms.[64]

Other phenotype characteristics like hair color, skin complexion, profile, facial bone structure, height, and natural voice tone are all generated from a genetic configuration unique to each individual. An individual's genetic configuration also reflects his or her predecessors' ethnic backgrounds.[65] Ethnicity incorporates culture, distinctions attributable to the effects of geographic region, a person's ancestry, and language. Imagine the chaos in a situation if all humans looked identical and could not distinguish between each other.

Among His proofs are the creation of the heavens and the earth, and the variations in your languages and your colors. In these, there are signs for the knowledgeable. (30:22)

O people, we created you from the same male and female, and rendered you distinct peoples and tribes, that you may recognize one another. The best among you in the sight of God is the most righteous. God is Omniscient, Cognizant. (49:13)

People describe themselves as having different "sides" to their personalities (e.g., a light side and a dark side, a good side and a bad side, a cooperative side and a contrary side). On the other hand, the proposition that an individual can have *distinct* multiple personalities is false.[66] The fact that each person is a single unique personality is clarified in the Quran.

"You have come back to us as individuals (furadaa), just as we created you the first time." (6:94, partial)

All of them will come before Him on the Day of Resurrection as individuals (far'daa). (19:95)

Let Me deal with one I created as an individual (khalaq'tu waheedaa). (74:11)

The phrases *furadaa* (6:94), *far'daa* (19:95), and *khalaq'tu waheedaa* (74:11) point out that a person is created as an individual and remains an individual. *Furadaa* means alone and solitary. *Far'daa* means single, alone and separate from others. *Waheedaa* means alone, single, unique, and separate from others. Even twins are unique individuals. Each twin has his or her own personality (*shakh'siah*). Each person meets with unique life circumstances tailored for the person's inner growth or lack of growth.

Psychospiritual Nature Proceeds from Spirit of God

Psychospiritual growth is the development of the human higher nature, a *nature from the spirit of God* blown into the human physical form. The word *human* is derived from the Sanskrit words *hu and manu. Hu* means "*Divine word or breath.*"[67] The Sanskrit word *manu* (or *manas*) refers to man, and means "*the one who thinks.*"[68] Thus, the word *human* denotes the attributes that distinguish humans from other creatures – spirit and mind. Both human attributes are noted in the Quran.

He shaped him and blew into him from His Spirit (Ruhihi). And He gave you the hearing, the eyesight, and the brains; rarely are you thankful. (32:9)

In the order of revelation, the first five Quran verses are:

Read, in the name of your Lord, who created. He created man from an embryo. Read, and your Lord, Most Exalted. Teaches by means of the pen. He teaches man what he never knew. (96:1-5)

The Creator instructed humans to examine, study, and understand the creation. Man is capable of carrying out the Divine instruction because there are two kinds of spirit that abide in humans. Descriptions of the spirits are limited to what God has revealed to man.

The *"human spirit"* (*Ar-Ruhu'l Insani*), analogous to the human mind or intelligence (not brain), distinguishes him [human] from the animal, and which is given to him, by the Decree of God, from heaven, of the true essence of which we know nothing. It is this spirit which is sometimes united to the body, and sometimes separated from it, as in sleep or death… The *"Exalted Spirit"* (*Ar-Ruhu 'l-Azam*) is connected with the existence of God, but the essence of which is unknown to all but the Almighty. The spiritual faculty in man…the original spirit of man first created by God.[69]

The *human spirit* (*Ar-Ruhu'l Insani*) and the *Exalted Spirit* (*Ar-Ruhu 'l-Azam*) are not the same. The human spirit or soul is "the one who thinks." Regardless of the extent of each individual's psychospiritual growth, the Exalted Spirit *always returns to God* when an individual departs from this life. Unlike the Exalted Spirit, the eternal habitat of a person's soul is largely determined by the extent of development of the "good side" of the person. On his or her own, no individual can merit the eternal blessing of returning and abiding in God's Presence (i.e., Heaven). The Creator enjoins humans to beseech Him alone for forgiveness and guidance. Analogous but not identical to physical development, psychospiritual growth takes place in ordered stages along a "difficult path" in life.

You will move from stage to stage (tabaqaan 'an tabaq). (84:19)

Did we not show him the two paths? He should choose the difficult path. Which one is the difficult path…? And being one of those who believe, and exhorting one another to be steadfast, and exhorting one another to be kind. These have deserved happiness. (90: 10-12, 17-18)

The soul and Him who created it. Then showed it what is evil and what is good. Successful is one who redeems (zakkahaa) it. Failing is one who neglects it. (91: 7-10)

Sheik Muhammad Qutb notes that personality development, reflected in the concept *taz'kiyah*, means:

Development of the good side of man and its promotion to the end of making him fulfill God's description of His creation in the best of forms…. Islamic development or growth, is equally fulfilled by the disciplining of the

SELF-KNOWLEDGE AND SPIRITUAL YEARNING

self (*nafs*) which is "capable of evil," by enabling it to master its affections and passions.[70]

Developing the "good side" or weaning away from blameworthy characteristics constitutes the "difficult path." Several psychologists and social scientists have promoted concepts similar to the "difficult path." Carl Rogers characterized this inner growth as "becoming a person."[71] Alfred Adler conceptualized it as the "unity of self," and "superiority feeling" (*not* superiority complex).[72] Victor Frankl said it is "taking responsibility to find the right answers" and "discovering the meaning of life."[73] Erik Erikson deemed it as attaining "integrity."[74] Abraham Maslow described it as "a hierarchy of needs" and moving towards "self-actualization."[75] Maslow later added another need to his hierarchy of needs beyond self-actualization, namely, "the need for transcendence." Maslow's need for transcendence roughly corresponds to the need for psychospiritual connection to the Spirit of God. Eric Fromm framed it as arriving at "beingness and freedom."[76]

Psychospiritual development involves actualizing noble, active, and spiritually dynamic qualities of the soul to please God.[77] By demonstrating sincere effort and discipline, a person becomes a content peaceful soul. Such effort and discipline is the *inner struggle* (*jihad un-nafs*) necessary for authentic self-actualization. *Jihad* involves: 1) confrontation with inclinations to embrace spiritually toxic thoughts and actions, and 2) learning how to discipline the false self that is "capable of evil." On his or her own, an individual cannot succeed in this struggle because an individual's "picture of the self" is never sufficiently honest and transparent enough to mirror all of the person's shortcomings and faults. In the absence of Divine inspiration and guidance, individuals are unwilling to face and do battle with their shortcomings, especially shortcomings that impede psychospiritual growth.

Psychospiritual development is reflected in a restoration of the self (*tajdeed un-nafs*) to merit return to the Creator's Presence. *Tajdeed* means "a renewal, rejuvenation, regeneration, and a refurbishing." Tajdeed also implies a return to *a previous state or condition*. Dawud Rosser-Owen points out:

[Tajdeed] is the process of renewal of the pristine form [i.e., pure form] of innate submission to God and inborn human nature within the individual and his close associates. The renewer (*majadid*) is the imam of the body, namely, the heart or mind acting under direction."[78]

Tajdeed is a conscious effort by an individual to advance his or her "good side" (*al-fit'ra*) in order to foster positive transformation. *This advance is a return of man to the nature that God created in him, a nature in harmony with Divine law.* A self that shies from this advance moves towards spiritual darkness and dismisses the "good side" that seeks self-knowledge. The self on the "good side" achieves self-knowledge, and is transformed, restored, and rejuvenated.

Only those who come to God with their whole heart (will be saved). (26:89)

If God renders one's heart content with Submission, he will be following a light from his Lord. Therefore, woe to those whose hearts are hardened against God's message; they have gone far astray. (39:22)

You Do Not Cause Anything

Once you decide to change, the Creator effectuates the change. In God's System, decisions and actions lead to outcomes, effects, and consequences. These truths reflect the laws of Absolute Divine Control, Limited Free Will, Personal Responsibility, and Relative Causality. You may (erroneously) think that, independent of the System, you literally *cause* a change to take place. To illustrate this error in thinking, hold a small object up in the air and release it. You are responsible for releasing the object but you did not *cause* the object to move downward. The object will fall owing to its properties and the law of gravity. You did not create the law of gravity or the properties of the object. You did not *cause* other forces to act on the object as it descended. The object (let's say a dish) broke upon hitting the floor. You are *responsible* for breaking the dish. Aware that dishes tend to break upon hitting the floor, you *decided* to release the dish in your hand. If you did not know anything about properties of dishes that make them easily breakable, you *still remain responsible*, although the breakage was *unintentional*. In a world subject to laws of gravity, relative causality, personal responsibility, and limited free will, others may ask, "Why did you break the dish?" Suppose you are in a gravity-free environment. Momentarily forgetting it is gravity-free, you decide to place a pencil on a desk fastened to the floor. The pencil floats. Your decision to set the pencil down is not in harmony with greater surrounding forces that prevent the pencil from settling on the table. A person's intentions and decisions are often *not* in harmony with the Truth. An individual's decisions and actions do not always yield a "good spiritual harvest." Nevertheless, God does not interfere with an individual's intentions and decisions, so as not to nullify limited free will and personal responsibility. An individual meets with the consequences of some of his or her actions. In His Mercy, God overlooks many actions.

It was not you who killed them; God is the One who killed them. It was not you who threw when you threw; God is the One who threw. But He thus gives the believers a chance to earn a lot of credit. God is Hearer, Omniscient. (8:17)

"This is a consequence of what your hands have sent forth. God is never unjust towards the creatures." (8:51)

…Thus, God does not change the condition of any people unless they themselves make the decision to change. If God wills any hardship for any people, no force can stop it. For they have none beside Him as Lord and Master. (13:11, partial)

All matters are controlled by Him from the heaven to the earth. To Him, the day is equivalent to one thousand of your years. (32:5)

Anything bad that happens to you is a consequence of your own deeds, and He overlooks many (of your sins). (42:30)

Cosmic Culture of Submission

Growth and development do not take place in a vacuum. The Creator revealed that the physical and psychological growth of human beings is similar to the growth of plants.

And God germinated you from the earth like plants. Then He returns you into it, and He will surely bring you out. (71:17-18)

Have you noted the crops you reap? Did you grow them, or did we? (56:63-64)

Verses 71:17-18 and 56:63-64 highlight the importance of culture in the growth of living things. God created and initiated the ongoing growth of plants and created the cultures conducive for growth. On the meaning of culture, Mir Valiuddin points out that:

Culture, as we know, is derived from the Latin word *cultura* and is primarily applicable to the cultivation of land and tillage.... But in the universal character of culture, be it flowers or of fruits, that what is important is the seed that is sown and the soil in which it is sown.... Nor, can the conditions which favor growth and development be neglected.[79]

In the human context, culture encompasses the social and psychological realms, including a person's values and ideals. In the context of the agricultural analogy, the seed is the inherent genetic characteristics of an individual. The soil is an individual's family, ever-changing social environment and psychological influences, and conditions that favor or impede wholesome personality development. Human culture includes the complete way of life and frame of reference for giving meaning to life. Humanity is provided with a Divinely ordained way of life to promote psychospiritual development. *Submission (aslama, Islam) to God alone is the religion and culture of creation.* Human beings have a revealed mode of worshipping the Creator Who makes it possible for humans to "grow" their souls. Individuals who sincerely worship God and lead a righteous life are not hamstrung by past mistakes and misdeeds. Their personalities mature in harmony with their worship of the Creator. To the extent that an individual's inner state and outer environment deviate from Submission, personality development is constrained.

The only religion approved by God is "Submission." Ironically, those who have received the scripture are the ones who dispute this fact, despite the knowledge they have received, due to jealousy. For such rejecters of God's revelations, God is most strict in reckoning. (3:19)

Are they seeking other than God's religion, when everything in the heavens and the earth has submitted to Him, willingly and unwillingly, and to Him they will be returned? (3:83)

As role models, parents inculcate their values and beliefs in their children. The family is the basic social unit in all cultures, and it is a microcosm of the larger society. Outside of family, an individual's associates, peers, and the general populace exert some influence on his or her character development. This relationship between cultural influences and an individual's values and beliefs has been confirmed by psychologists and anthropologists. The reciprocal relationship between an individual's personality and preferred social groups is reflected in the adage, "You can tell a man by the company he keeps." It is important to frequent the company of individuals who share a similar spiritual yearning for the truth; however, a person does not need to separate from individuals who do not specifically share the person's same spiritual creed. It is necessary to exercise discretion in choosing associates in order to guard against negative psychospiritual influences. Dr. Carl Jung pointed out that the absence of God consciousness in a society ushers in the moral deterioration of its members and retards their psychospiritual development:

> If dull people lose the idea of God, nothing happens—not immediately and personally at least. But socially the masses begin to breed mental epidemics, of which we now have a fair number.[80]

Any ultra-materialistic irreligious culture gives rise to all kinds of psychological illnesses, emotional problems, and maladjustments (e.g., family breakdown, sexual promiscuity and disorders, alcohol and drug abuse, anxiety and depression, and violence). The widespread occurrence of "neurotic" personalities is the end result. From the perspective of submission to God, many societies that are referred to as "developed" are immature in respect to psychospiritual growth. No community has been without righteous guides and teachers to help its people turn towards Truth. Messengers of God received inspiration and direction that enabled them to counsel their contemporaries. Prophets of God received Divine revelation. In their capacities as servants of God, *all* prophets and messengers reflect an ideal pattern of behavior. People with positive spiritual yearnings are idealists in varying degrees. The true ideal pattern (*sunna*) is Submission to God. God created mankind and the ideal pattern for humanity to follow in harmony with Divine law. More people are discovering that their perception of Submission (i.e., Islam) is distorted partly because of centuries of indoctrination by ill-informed clergy and the introduction of dogma into Islam. Submission (Islam) is an all-encompassing Divinely ordained way of life that transcends any particular society and time. The culture of Islam among humans is man-implemented but not man-made.

The Submitter Personality

The Submitter Personality is characterized by: 1) an active spiritual yearning to obey and please God, 2) non-allegiance to any person, group, belief, or cause counter to God's guidance and commands, and 3) courage to relinquish false doctrines.

Being a submitter to God does not make an individual immune from the emotional and psychological vicissitudes of life. Far from feeling burdened, individuals who acquire a Submitter Personality experience a sense of purpose, soundness of mind, and psychospiritual peace. These and other characteristics are synthesized in verse 98:7.

Those who believed and led a righteous life are the best creatures. (98:7)

[N]othing can happen to me, unless my Lord wills it. My Lord's knowledge encompasses all things. Would you not take heed? "Why should I fear your idols? It is you who should be afraid, since you worship instead of God idols that are utterly powerless to help you. Which side is more deserving of security, if you know?" Those who believe, and do not pollute their belief with idol worship, have deserved the perfect security, and they are truly guided. Such was our argument, with which we supported Abraham against his people. We exalt whomever we will to higher ranks. Your Lord is Most Wise, Omniscient. (6:80, 83 partial)

Prophet Abraham's journey to the understanding that only God should be worshipped is a beautiful example of psychospiritual personality development. Using his God-given intelligence and reason and remaining sensitive to the inner Exalted Spirit, Abraham first distanced himself from his family and community's false beliefs and practices. He chose not to be satisfied with the status quo of the time. Abraham was not content with mirroring his contemporaries' definition of a "healthy, normal personality." Unafraid, he sought the truth about the source of life. In so doing, his need for spiritual transcendence beyond the "created" was satisfied. For Abraham, self-realization and the worship of God were inseparable. Through his resolute search to realize the inner Divine connection, Abraham, by God's will, gave us the *Submitter Personality*—the human who submits to God alone. The soul or real person is focused on the True Reality.

IV

Darkness, Shadows, And Light

The task of the self is to realize that nothing is self-subsistent except God. If this is difficult for a mature person to grasp, the person has yet to discover that he or she lacks true self-awareness. Many people erroneously believe that that they know who they are. From birth, people tell each other who they think they are and what they expect from each other. Each individual tells others what he or she expects from them and how he or she wants to be viewed. *Mutual agreement between an individual and others as to the individual's perceived real self may not reflect the truth.*

True self-awareness is the fruit of genuine spiritual yearning. Self-deception and ignorance are outcomes of an uncultivated spiritual yearning, i.e., the lack of a desire to please the Creator. To understand personality is to understand that this spiritual yearning is a critical element of personality development. Most people follow conjecture and guess about this important matter. The Creator revealed the truth about this matter for our benefit. An individual must go beyond convention and mundane matters to attain self-knowledge.

If you obey the majority of people on earth, they will divert you from the path of God. They follow only conjecture; they only guess. Your Lord is fully aware of those who stray off His path, and He is fully aware of those who are guided. (6:116-117)

Each soul was made aware of an assignment given to it prior to its descent into this world. Each soul chooses to seek the Source, or it becomes overly absorbed in this fleeting world. A *jinn* (descendent of Satan) is matched with each human born in this world. If a person thinks that he or she knows himself or herself without Divine guidance, the person is making a serious mistake. Can you imagine a droplet of water that is not motivated to reunite with the sea from whence it came? The droplet assumes many forms (i.e., ice, rain, and mist) as it transverses fleeting states on its way back to the sea. Because their development is preconfigured and predetermined, caterpillars become moths and butterflies. Because its development is preconfigured and predetermined, a small seed may germinate and grow into a huge oak tree. Caterpillars and seeds do not have a choice in this matter. Humans have a choice. Individuals can choose to utilize their intelligence and inborn sense of a Higher Being to facilitate psychospiritual growth or join the crowd that seldom tires of engaging in conjecture and guesswork. Unlike the predetermined motivation of a seed or caterpillar, each person must be inspired to pursue personal growth. Personal motivation to change remains insufficient until a person believes that he or she has drifted too far from a desired ideal. Individuals who genuinely seek self-knowledge realize that the desired ideal is *actualization in submission to God.*

Spiritual Darkness

In this discourse, there are three levels of self-awareness: darkness, shadows, and light. Souls immersed in complete spiritual darkness (*zulmah*) are intoxicated with this world and oblivious to the purpose of life. Such individuals dim the inner intuitive spiritual light that transcends physical and mental sensation. As the darkness of falsehood and deception shrouding the self (*an-nafs*) intensifies, the person loses spiritual yearning and embraces evil. The person becomes an evildoer (*zallaam*).

Their example is like those who start a fire, then, as it begins to shed light around them, God takes away their light, leaving them in darkness, unable to see. (2:17)

In total spiritual darkness, the lost estranged self (A*n-nafs ath-thala)* has chosen misguidance and deception (*tath'leel*) instead of God's guidance. The lost estranged self is not concerned about deviating from the right *spiritual* path; the estranged self thinks that it is guided, thinks that it has the right perspective on life, and thinks that it knows the "right answers." Satisfied in deviating from God's guidance, this self is mad or possessed (*maj'nun*).

Say, "Shall we implore, beside God, what possesses no power to benefit us or hurt us, and turn back on our heels after God has guided us? In that case, we would join those possessed by the devils (as'tah'rat'hu shaeyaateen), and rendered utterly confused (hairana), while their friends try to save them: 'Stay with us on the right path.'" Say, "God's guidance is the right guidance. We are commanded to submit to the Lord of the universe.'" (6:71)

The devil (ash-shaetaan) has possessed them (as'tah'waza alayhim), and has caused them to disregard God's message. These are the party of the devil. Absolutely, the party of the devil are the losers. (58:19)

Allegiance to the evil self leads to preoccupation with adornment and material attachment. Subjects of the evil self believe that the "good life" is solely reflected in physical indulgence and material possession. Modesty in adornment, modest satisfaction of physical appetites, and the desire for ample provisions are natural and healthy. The evil self encourages a person, via his or her actions and thoughts, to say, "There is nothing worthy of worship except me and what I desire and find acceptable." Such individuals' limited knowledge is of no ultimate benefit to them; they stunt their spiritual growth and dwarf their souls.

Have you noted the one whose God is his ego? Consequently, God sends him astray, despite his knowledge, seals his hearing and his mind, and places a veil on his eyes. Who then can guide him, after such a decision by God? Would you not take heed? (45:23)

Allegiance to the evil self leads to psychospiritual blindness. The evil self makes its subjects blind to their spiritual blindness. They "see light" where there is none. The "light" that they see is a false perception of themselves as enlightened and aware of what is important in life. The evil self encourages a person to fabricate and promote slander and rumor, commit unrighteous acts, and violate the reserve of modesty. Violations of modesty and unrighteous acts are deemed as uninhibited expressions of personal freedom. Subjects of the evil self elevate their views and opinions above guidance from God.

Had we willed, we could have elevated him therewith, but he insisted on sticking to the ground, and pursued his own opinions. Thus, he is like the dog; whether you pet him or scold him, he pants. Such is the example of people who reject our proofs. Narrate these narrations, that they may reflect. (7:176)

Another allegory is that of being in total darkness in the midst of a violent ocean, with waves upon waves, in addition to thick fog. Darkness upon darkness—if he looked at his own hand, he could barely see it. Whomever God deprives of light, will have no light. (24:40)

The "Hand" in the Verse of Darkness

God informs humans that when He removes His Light, there is no light. The unbelievers' state is described as "Depths of darkness…one above another." Unbelievers as described in verse 24:40 are akin to mariners at sea under starless night skies in vessels with no light of their own. The evildoer (*zallaam*) or sojourner plunges deeper into spiritual darkness. The sojourner is described in the verse as barely able to see his or her hand.

In verse 24:40, "hand" is also a metaphor for self-identification and human activity. Following are some of the metaphorical meanings of "hand" in the verse:

1. *The hand is the external organ of inscription, activity, and civilization.* Written expression is more permanent than speech alone. Human civilization has progressed from drawing crude pictures on the face of stones to the manufacture of artificial intelligence (e.g., computer technologies). We have erected mammoth libraries filled with volumes of the written word. This accomplishment is an obvious proof that human beings are endowed with intelligence and abilities beyond the reach and ability of other creatures. Persons *governed* by the evil self use their faculties to promote falsehood. They compose theories, philosophies, and "evidence" to support their beliefs. They erect psychological mechanisms to debunk God consciousness and capture others in the grip of spiritual darkness.

2. *The hand is a symbol of power.* Righteous individuals realize that any power in this world is a blessing from God that should be used to advance the welfare of humanity. True power is a God-given opportunity and potential to promote positive enterprises. In contrast, spiritually blind individuals view power as proceeding from themselves. They are arrogant and exploit others who they deem beneath them. Individuals governed by the evil self become intoxicated with worldly power and influence. They attempt to evade the One Who is All-Powerful *(Al-Muqtadir).*

3. *The hand is used to point, guide, and direct.* People enslaved to the evil self are misguided and misguide others. Their deeds are distant from the path of righteousness (*as-sirat al-mustaqeem*) that constitutes wholesome personality development. These individuals do not recognize that they are "off course" and removed from God's guidance. The lack of direction is self-imposed. Imagine being in a completely dark cave grasping the hands of others. No one knows the proper direction. Yet, each insists that he or she is guided.

4. *The hand is used to reach out, touch, and grasp.* Like an injured hand that no longer functions properly, the minds of spiritually blind individuals are unable to grasp or retain spiritual truths. Their rejection of truth renders them incapable of helping others discover the meaning of life.

The minds and hearts of the spiritually blind are emptied of genuine spiritual yearning. Such persons are diagnosed and described in the Quran as *"diseased in their minds,"* (i.e., mentally ill).

In their minds there is a disease (marad). Consequently, God augments their disease (maradaa). They have incurred a painful retribution for their lying. (2:10)

The devil has possessed them, and has caused them to disregard God's message. These are the party of the devil. Absolutely, the party of the devil are the losers. (58:10)

The Root of Psychospiritual Darkness

Conceit *(kibr)* is self-worship and the root of spiritual darkness. The twelfth century Muslim philosopher Al-Ghazzali said, conceit is "a feeling of superiority in the mind whereby a person places him or her self above others."[81] Externalized conceit is arrogance *(takabbar),* immodest pride visible to others. Conceit includes *undeserving* self-regard. A conceited person believes that he or she should *not* be held accountable to the same canons as others. In order to maintain a routine of self-adoration and self-veneration, the person constantly dismisses truths that contradict his or her conceited outlook and behavior. The most important dismissed fact is that only God is worthy of worship. Conceit and arrogance reflect the perversion of the natural inclination to worship God. Arrogance includes the characteristics of refusal, heedlessness, and rejection.

Children Are Naturally Self-Centered

What may appear to be self-centered behavior in small children is not conceit. Responsible parents teach their children modesty and concern for others as their children grow from the toddler stage to pre-adolescence. Newborns and small children "demand" that *their* needs and desires are met. Such behavior is normal and a necessary condition for survival.[82] Toddlers perceive the world from their limited perspective. Concerned about survival and satisfaction, a small child is not old enough to contemplate being treated as an exception to rules, being superior to others, or the idea of "self-love."

Introduced in traditional Psychoanalytic Theory, the concept of "infantile narcissim" is a myth. The term, narcissism, has been adopted to describe immature self-centered adult behavior. A mythical character in Greek folklore, Narcissus looked into a pool of water and fell in love with his own image. No infant or toddler can fall in love with his or her own image. If anything, an infant or toddler is fascinated with his or her reflection in water or in a mirror, possibly wandering what the image is.

When they cannot have their way, children exhibit resistance, become heedless, and act as if their parents have rejected or no longer love them. In psychospiritually healthy individuals, the selfish, self-centered child matures into a considerate adult. Teaching his son behavior conducive to a healthy personality, Prophet Luqman said:

"O my son, you shall observe the Contact Prayers (Salat). You shall advocate righteousness and forbid evil, and remain steadfast in the face of adversity. These are the most honorable traits. You shall not treat the people with arrogance, nor shall you roam the earth proudly. God does not like the arrogant showoffs. Walk humbly and lower your voice—the ugliest voice is the donkey's voice." (31:17-19)

Satan: Father of Conceit

Iblis[83] was the first creature to express conceit and arrogance when he did not heed God's command to the angels to prostrate before Adam. When Iblis rebelled against God, he became *Satan (Shaitan - "one who is rejected or cast out")*. Blaming God instead of himself for his downfall, Satan proclaimed his desire to deceive and destroy human souls. Despite his pontifications, Satan is eternally subservient to God.

When we said to the angels, "Fall prostrate before Adam," they fell prostrate, except Satan; he refused, was too arrogant (istak'bara), and a disbeliever. (2:34)

God has condemned him [Satan], and he said, "I will surely recruit a definite share of Your worshipers. I will mislead them, I will entice them, I will command them to (forbid the eating of certain meats by) marking the ears of livestock, and I will command them to distort the creation of God." (4:118)

Arrogant conceited individuals worship an evil self that abides inside each one of them. When Satan is a person's confidante, the person loses his or her psychospiritual balance. In his or her aversion to moral choices, the person imitates Satan when he rebelled against God. The conceited ego-driven self *chooses* to indulge Satan. In the Quran, such individuals are also described as: "having refusing hearts," "given to sin", "fleeing from truth," "obstinate," "hemmed in by their own schemes," and "haughty." Conditions in this life provide individuals with a steady stream of opportunities to exercise their limited free will in concert with or in opposition to Divine guidance. Those who exercise their will according to God's guidance are protected from Satan's whispers (*was'wasi*).

Main Branch of Spiritual Darkness

Branches of spiritual darkness extend from excessive devotion and attachment to any idea, any enterprise, anything, or anyone other than God. The Arabic word *shirk* means "to add, include, or attach something to." In the spiritual context, shirk refers to the inclination to rely on or worship anything or anyone besides God. *Shirk is idolatry.* In the English dictionary, the original meaning of the word has been modified; the revised English meaning is "to avoid" as in avoiding (shirking) responsibility.[84] By avoiding the responsibility to worship the One God, many people practice shirk.

Shirk-ul-'Ilm is the act of ascribing knowledge in an absolute sense to a source other than God. Any innate or learned knowledge that a creature is entrusted with comes from God. God alone is All-Knowing. His Knowledge is not derived from anything nor is His Knowledge deficient in any way. Immersed in limited worldly knowledge, unbelievers do not benefit from intuitive or revealed knowledge about God or the purpose of life. Some of them claim to have knowledge that is the preserve of God. Suppressing their spiritual yearning, unbelievers' knowledge is of no use in growing their eternal souls. Unbelievers embrace false "facts" about the purpose of life in order to maintain an illusion of mental security.

God: there is no other God besides Him, the Living, the Eternal. Never a moment of unawareness or slumber overtakes Him. To Him belongs everything in the heavens and everything on earth. Who could intercede with Him, except in accordance with His will? He knows their past, and their future. No one attains any knowledge, except as He wills. His dominion encompasses the heavens and the earth, and ruling them never burdens Him. He is the Most High, the Great. (2:255)

Among the people, there are those who argue about God without knowledge, and follow every rebellious devil. (22:3)

Shirk-ut-Tasarruf is the belief that anyone or anything shares power, control, and influence with God. The concept of intercessors with God is the most common form of idolatry. The most pervasive institutionalized example of idolatry is the belief that someone or something shares power, control, influence, or even is "part" of God. Other examples are idolatrous belief in faith healers, saints, and persons who seek to be regarded by others as having powers belonging to God. Some individuals erroneously believe that God does not have full control of affairs in this world. God controls all matters, all creatures, life and death, the minds and hearts of people, each individual, time (past, present, and future), all forces and natural laws, the movement of heavenly bodies, anything smaller than an atom or mustard seed, day and night, the condition of people, all provisions for His entire creation, and the Hereafter.[85]

Absolutely, the religion shall be devoted to God alone. Those who set up idols beside Him say, "We idolize them only to bring us closer to God; for they are in a better position!" God will judge them regarding their disputes. God does not guide such liars, disbelievers. (39:3)

Shirk-ul'Adah is commitment to concocted rituals, beliefs, superstitions, and rites that are said to bring about good or bad circumstances. For example, some individuals believe that the number thirteen is a sign of harm or misfortune. Black cats, black birds (ravens), and black dogs are associated with evil. Figurines, statuettes, motifs, and certain pictures believed to ward off evil and misfortune adorn motor vehicles, doorways, and homes. Some people engage in ritual behavior during certain phases of the moon or during the apparent "movement" of the sun in the sky, light candles to invoke spirits, wear certain colors, stones, metals, and jewelry as body shields and in order to invoke positive vibrations.

They pursued what the devils taught concerning Solomon's kingdom. Solomon, however, was not a disbeliever, but the devils were disbelievers. They taught the people sorcery, and that which was sent down through the two angels of Babel, Haroot and Maroot. These two did not divulge such knowledge without pointing out: "This is a test. You shall not abuse such knowledge." But the people used it in such evil schemes as the breaking up of marriages. They can never harm anyone against the will of God. They thus learn what hurts them, not what benefits them, and they know full well that whoever practices witchcraft will have no share in the Hereafter. Miserable indeed is what they sell their souls for, if they only knew. (2:102)

Confused Self in Shadows

The Confused Wandering Self *(An Nafs Ad-Dalla)* veers off the right spiritual path. The self is uncertain about the purpose of life. In this condition, the heart is sincere but the person is subject to control by his or her physical appetites and other distractions. The self becomes attached to one appearance and then another one. Like an unsteady vessel, the person wavers and vacillates *(mutaqallib)* between spiritual darkness and light. This self remembers God depending on the circumstances. Unlike the evil self enveloped in complete spiritual darkness, the confused self still wants to please God. Out of weakness, the self may *cling* to misdeeds *(zulaamat)*. The thoughts that give birth to such misdeeds are like regions of darkness *(zulam)* in the inner self. An individual may not be initially aware that such thoughts and behavior are spiritually toxic. Once a person understands the nature of such behavior, he or she seeks refuge in the light of God's guidance. God guides the sincere person to the realization that nothing, including self-consciousness, exists independent of God.

This self acknowledges its misdeeds, asks God for forgiveness, does not repeat wrongdoings, and seeks repose in the Mercy of God. Almighty God guides the wandering self away from practices born of error, ignorance, and falsehood because no one but God is able to fully overpower the evil forces.

There are others who have confessed their sins; they have mixed good deeds with bad deeds. God will redeem them, for God is Forgiver, Most Merciful (9:102)

Healthy Personalities Thrive in the Light of Truth

The Truth is the Light that removes the cover of darkness and ignorance from our souls. In the light of reflected Truth, a person can distinguish the real from the unreal, and the true from the false. God is the Absolute Light (*An-Nur*) and the Absolute Truth (*Al-Haqq*). Obviously, no creature can see God, but provided the heart is sincere, a person can see God's Truth and Light reflected in the inner self and in creation.

God is the light of the heavens and the earth. The allegory of His light is that of a concave mirror behind a lamp that is placed inside a glass container. The glass container is like a bright, pearl-like star. The fuel thereof is supplied from a blessed oil-producing tree, that is neither eastern, nor western. Its oil is almost self-radiating; needs no fire to ignite it. Light upon light. God guides to His light whoever wills (to be guided). God thus cites the parables for the people. God is fully aware of all things. (24:35)

In his famous treatise entitled *Mishkat Al Anwar*,[86] the fifth century (according to the Islamic calendar) philosopher and mystic Abu Hamid al-Ghazzali made several important distinctions between physical sight and human intellect. He discussed the grades of human consciousness in the allegorical context of light and darkness. Light symbolizes consciousness, intelligence, guidance, and the ultimate True Reality. Darkness symbolizes ignorance, unconsciousness, illusion, falsehood, evil, and blindness to Truth. Al-Ghazzali eloquently conveyed the beauty of this allegory as it relates to psychospiritual development.

First, physical light is visible and makes other things visible. The human physical eye receives physical light. Although unparalleled in design and ability, the human eye has certain limitations: 1) the human eye cannot see things far away or extremely close, 2) the eye cannot see itself, 3) the eye cannot see objects hidden behind other objects, 4) the eye cannot see the inner qualities of things, 5) the eye cannot see in the dark, and 6) the eye cannot see all visible physical light. In the modern age via special instruments, humans can see infrared and ultraviolet light).

In contrast to the physical eye, the inner eye or intelligence can: 1) grasp what is distant in time and space, 2) see or know itself (self-consciousness), 3) perceive that which is hidden behind objects or veils, 4) fathom the inner qualities of things, 5) apprehend things independent of physical light, and 6) transcend physical dimensions. This comparison between physical vision and physical light on one hand and the inner eye of intelligence on the other points out that human consciousness is not caused by sensory-perceptual processes. Often labeled as objective reality, the physical world is at most an opaque shadow of True Reality. Spiritual yearners seek the True Reality, but spiritually stifled souls are oblivious to evidence of the greater Reality. Indeed, these two views of reality lead to distinct conceptions of the self and its development.

If God renders one's heart content with Submission, he will be following a light from his Lord. Therefore, woe to those whose hearts are hardened against God's message; they have gone far astray. (39: 22)

Clearly, the inner eye and its light are far superior to physical sight and its light. According to Al-Ghazzali, comparing inner light with physical light is like comparing light with abject darkness. God is the Light that makes all else visible and invisible. Man is presented with proofs throughout creation to open the inner eye of his intelligence and soul. The proofs include revealed reminders that God alone is The Reality (*Al-Haqq*). The self has no light (knowledge) short of what is revealed and inspired in the self. The submitting self may be given a momentary "glimpse" of the *reflected* Reality and, as a result, will seek all that can be retained from the "glimpse."

No visions can encompass Him, but He encompasses all visions. He is the Compassionate, the Cognizant. Enlightenments have come to you from your Lord. As for those who can see, they do so for their own good, and those who turn blind, do so to their own detriment. I am not your guardian. (6: 103-104)

A "mountain peak" exits in each person, and the peak is the ego, born of false beliefs and perceptions (veils) of this world. Perceived as separate from all else, the ego must be humbled and eventually eliminated. In this life, we rely upon our limited knowledge and naïve sense of independence as supports, as did Moses when he gazed upon Mount Horeb (identified with Mount Sinai). God spoke to Moses and said, "If it stays in its place, then you can see Me." God caused the mountain to crumble, and Moses as a conscious self apart from the Reality could not behold the Divine manifestation. The self has no consciousness outside of consciousness granted by the Creator. When a person realizes that his or her soul is from God, the person understands that the ego-self has no existence on its own. The most harmful psychospiritual state is the self's insistence that it is apart from, unheedful of, and independent of God, the Absolute Light (*An-Nur*).

You shall not worship beside God any other god. There is no other god beside Him. Everything perishes except His presence. To Him belongs all sovereignty, and to Him you will be returned. (28:88)

Spiritual enlightenment comes when a person realizes that to God alone belongs all worship. God lights an invisible spiritual "wick" of self-consciousness. The person realizes that his or her perceptions and knowledge are at best mere flickers of opaque reflections from the One Who lights all else and is not lighted by any other. What seems to be controlled and initiated by others including the self is actually the Will and Command of God. It is God's Will that humans have a limited free will and relative control.

"I have put my trust in God, my Lord and your Lord. There is not a creature that He does not control. My Lord is on the right path. (11:56)

The mind apprehends relative causes, effects, and changes in this spatial-temporal dimension. The Command of God is *far* superior to this lowly dimension. Like Prophet Abraham, a mature psychospiritual person knows who and what he or she is, is aware of the Creator, and seeks forgiveness from the Creator.

"[F]or I am devoted only to the Lord of the universe. The One who created me, and guided me. The One who feeds me and waters me. And when I get sick, He heals me. The One who puts me to death, then brings me back to life. The One who hopefully will forgive my sins on the Day of Judgment. My Lord, grant me wisdom, and include me with the righteous. Let the example I set for the future generations be a good one. Make me one of the inheritors of the blissful Paradise." *(26: 77 partial - 85)*

A beacon of light revealed by God, the Quran presents God's guidance to those who have the spiritual vision and yearning to benefit from its message. In order to benefit from Revelatory light, the soul must yearn for it.

O you who believe, you shall reverence God and believe in His messenger. He will then grant you double the reward from His mercy, endow you with light (nur) to guide you, and forgive you. God is Forgiver, Most Merciful. (57: 28)

The Creator taught Adam the 'names' (i.e., names and nature of all creatures, select forces, man's inventions, and other things human beings encounter while on Earth) so that, endowed with knowledge, Adam, Eve, and their guided descendents could carry out the Divine trust given to them.

He taught Adam all the names then presented them to the angels, saying, "Give me the names of these, if you are right." They said, "Be You glorified, we have no knowledge, except that which You have taught us. You are the Omniscient, Most Wise." (2:31-32)

Revelation is a light that enables man's consciousness to transverse beyond the apparent to the Real. Man needs to know what the Creator expects of him while he travels along this life path. The illuminated soul matriculates from one light to another until the soul is absorbed in the Light of God. Dr. Syed Abdul-Latif wrote:

The yearning for light has to begin in this life; and this is possible only for those who feel what is called *huzar-al-qalb,* or *the sense of God in every situation.*[87] (italics added)

Huzar-al-qalb gives direction to the inspired self in all situations. This sense of God is a safeguard against a tyranny of negative, debilitating mood states and behavior.

Meditation

Meditation involves *focusing* individual attention or consciousness. Any sensation or thought can be the focus of a person's attention, but meditation includes *remembering* the object of focus. Willful repeated focus on a sensation or thought soon becomes automatic and emerges in the mind without effort. When a person places a magnifying glass between a *light* source and a flammable surface, and adjusts the distances appropriately, the surface will start to burn. The burn occurs as a result of the *concentration* of light and heat rays on a single point on the flammable surface. Human beings are prefitted for focused concentration and meditation. In his book, *Contemplation,* Dr. Malik Badri notes:

Contemplation then makes use of all the cognitive activities employed by a human being in the thinking processes. However, it differs from secular in-depth thinking in that its visions and concepts go beyond this world of the here and now to encounter infinite dimensions of the hereafter; its object goes from the creation to the Creator.... [T]he power of concentration has a biological basis in the human nervous system, and that it lies in the reticular formation and activating system. This formation, which is situated at the stem of the brain, acts as a gate controlling the nervous pulses and stimuli which go up to the higher centers of the brain.[88]

The *ultimate positive thought* that a person can have is thinking about God and His attributes.

O you who believe, you shall remember God frequently. You shall glorify Him day and night. (33:41-42)

For example, some people meditate on Oneness, Unity, Harmony, and Peace. Concentration on positive thoughts has a calming positive effect on the mind and the body. Conversely, frequent negative thoughts and feelings increase irritability, stress, and illness. Numerous research studies indicate a significant relationship between chronic mental stress and a lowered physical immune system. Thoughts can help heal, and thoughts can help kill. Meditation requires self-discipline and patience because the mind must be free of competing thoughts and urges. Once the mind is free of distractions, a person can tune his or her created consciousness to the Uncreated Consciousness (e.g., God). The highest form of meditation is concentrated spiritual remembrance (*dhikr*) of God, the Exalted Spirit. This remembrance or connection has an incalculable, illuminating, and embracing effect on the mind, body, and soul.

The yearning for this connection arises in souls who seek God and the reflections of His Light in their lives. Referring to this enrapturing state of consciousness, Dr. R.M. Bucke stated:

> The man who has the cosmic sense for even a few minutes only, will probably never again descend to the spiritual level of a merely conscious man; but twenty, thirty, or forty years afterwards, he will still feel within him the purifying, strengthening, and exalting effect of the divine illumination....[89]

Allegorically speaking, the soul is like a lamp that God has placed in the middle of a room. The room reflects the entirety of a person, including the person's perception of reality. Light in the lamp enables the person to see what is in the room. Individuals dim or cover the light but claim to see what is in their rooms. Each time a person intentionally forgoes an opportunity to remember and worship God, their light dims. Each time an individual evasively credits someone or something in the room with a mercy granted by God, their light dims. Each time an individual decides that someone or something in the room deserves greater priority than heeding God's command, their light dims. The more light is veiled, the more impaired is the person's vision in the room. The more light the person receives, the more the person can see God's signs in the room called life. There are no innocent souls in any rooms.

The earth is full of signs for those who are certain. And within yourselves; can you see? In the heaven is your provision, and everything that is promised to you. By the Lord of the heaven and the earth, this is as true as the fact that you speak. (51:20-23)

Fueled from its Divine source, the inner *light brightens* and an individual realizes that all glory and praise belong to the One Who created humanity, the light, the lamp, the room, and everything else. An inspired person lets the light burn bright by not attempting to snuff a single thought about God and His attributes out of his or her mind. When a person *seeks the light itself* and not just what the light makes visible, the person can distinguish between what is fleeting and the true Reality. A person who *purposely* blocks or dims the light, certainly is not seeking it. The *highest meditation* is to learn to love the Light Source of all things. Remember Abraham? He scanned his room. He questioned statues venerated by his people. He looked towards the heavens. He communicated with the Light Source. As a result of his Submitter Personality, Abraham sought actualization in the worship and adoration of God.

As a child, I was intrigued by moths' incessant efforts to make contact with physical light, even at the expense of inflicting injury upon themselves. I repeatedly turned a light switch on and off, just to watch moths return to the light, bounce off a lampshade, and make additional attempts to reach the light source. The glow of the light was not enough for them; they wanted to make contact with the light *source*. As I grew older and gained knowledge about the True Reality, I wondered why most humans do not seek the Light Source.

The expression, "all praise belongs to God," is much broader and deeper in significance than "I praise God." An individual can only praise God according to what the person knows or believes is in his or her room. No individual can see everything in the room, nor can a person see outside of the room. "All praise belongs to God" comprises both the kind of praise that man is aware of and the praise that man is unaware of. *A healthy personality praises God.* The praise need not be audible, visible, or discernable to any other than the One to whom it is intended. Inspired souls yearn for the Praise to reverberate in every cell of their being. Only advancing souls can withstand the Creator's Presence and Light.

The day will come when you see the believing men and women with their lights radiating ahead of them and to their right. Good news is yours that, on that day, you will have gardens with flowing streams. You will abide therein forever. This is the great triumph. On that day, the hypocrite men and women will say to those who believed, "Please allow us to absorb some of your light." It will be said, "Go back behind you, and seek light." A barrier will be set up between them, whose gate separates mercy on the inner side, from retribution on the outer side. (57: 12-13)

No language is superior to others when it comes to praising God. Created with a limited free will, humans are commanded to glorify God, thereby giving the correct healthy expression of spiritual yearning. In the absence of this praise, a person glorifies himself or herself and reverences what the Light makes visible in the room.

Extol your Lord. (74:3)

Glorify the name of your Lord, the Most High. He creates and shapes. He designs and guides. (87: 1-3)

V

Psychospiritual Development

Human Connection to the Existence of God

Contact or connection with the Lord of creation is the essential lifeline for psychospiritual growth. *God blew His Spirit (Ruhi) into the human being.* The original Exalted Spirit (*Ar-Ruhu 'l-Azam*) that dwells in each person is *connected* with the existence of God. The Spirit is not God or a "piece" of God, just as photons or rays of sunlight are *not* the sun itself. As long as the sun or light source shines, photons of light appear. In the absence of the light source, there is no light. The connection between God and the human Exalted Spirit is strengthened by making spiritual contact to God through prayer. Without this contact, the physical body matures, but the spirit-soul, the real person, slowly withers. The "Exalted Spirit" is nourished through contact and connection to the Divine Existence from whence it came. This is the most abiding unalterable sense of security and safety. The real self (i.e., soul) is from the breath of God and needs to maintain contact with the Existence of God. *This is the core of self-knowledge.* Derived from the word *nasiya*, the words *nasu* and *anasahum* (verse 59:19) mean "to neglect, to forget, or fall into oblivion." One consequence of neglecting or denying the connection to the Existence of God is free-falling into a state of inner oblivion or *existential anxiety*, a seemingly unshakable doubt about the reality of existence. God prevents anyone who staunchly chooses to forget God and ignore His proofs from attaining self-knowledge. The denier does not gain entry into realities (e.g., signs and proofs of the existence of God, the Unseen) that he or she insists do not exist.

Do not be like those who forgot God (nasu wa Allaha), so He made them forget themselves (fa'a nasahum an' fusahum). These are the wicked. (59:19)

Emanating from the spiritual domain (Ruh), the real self (soul) makes use of a mind (psychospiritual domain), and a body (physical domain) including a brain and senses. By receiving and processing sensory input, the real self engages and experiences this world (i.e., physical life). The self interfaces with physical reality, and individual personality development occurs in the psychospiritual domain of consciousness.

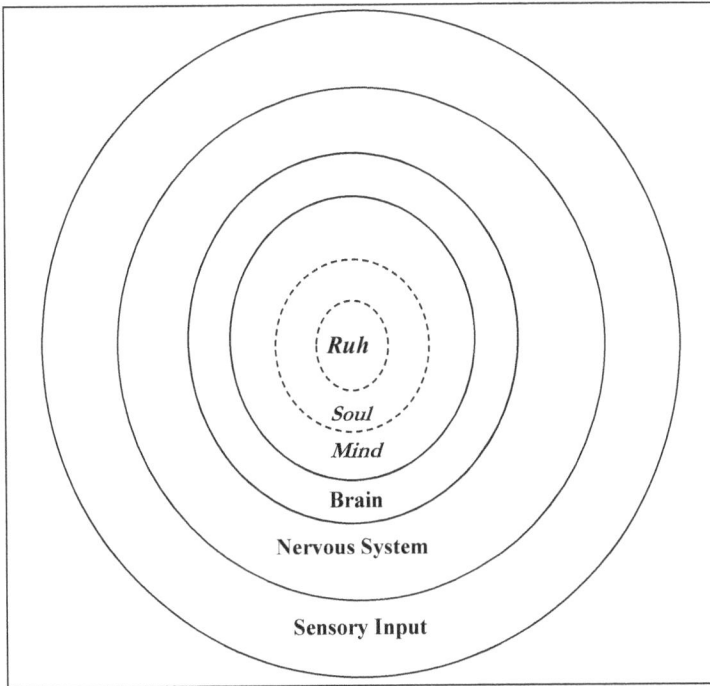

Figure 5.1. Domains of Human Consciousness

Psychospiritual contact and connection with the Spirit of God are as light, water, and air are to the life and growth of a plant. Nothing in this world can nourish or sustain the Exalted Spirit that dwells in each person. Even in the absence of *conscientious* connection (through prayer and worship), the Exalted Spirit does not wither or die. In spiritual darkness, the soul of a wicked person "shrinks" and does not grow. The person's spiritual yearning wanes. Human consciousness emanates from the human spirit (*Ar-Ruhu'l Insani*). The human spirit remains in the physical body until the time of death and vacates the body during sleep and loss of consciousness.

Development Occurs in Stages

In the Quran, human physical development is compared to the growth of plants[90] as reflected in the word *nabata*. The development takes place in lawful stages (*at'waraa*). Over fourteen centuries ago, the stages of human prenatal physical development were described in precise detail in the Quran[91]: 1) lodgment in the earth i.e., clay, 2) quintessence in male spermatozoa and female egg, 3) placement in the mother's womb, and 4) formation of physical form. At a critical point including conception onward (known only by God), the life in the womb becomes another creature—a creature into whom God has breathed His Spirit.

Why should you not strive to reverence God? He is the One who created you in stages (at'waraa)... And God germinated you (anbatakum) from the earth like plants (nabata). (71:13-14, 17)

Then we developed the drop into a hanging (embryo), then developed the hanging (embryo) into a bite-size (fetus), then created the bite-size (fetus) into bones, then covered the bones with flesh. We thus produce a new creature. Most blessed is God, the Best Creator. (23:14)

Following birth, each person physically matures, dies, and is raised from the dead on the Last Day. There is considerably more to human life than physical maturation and death. This "more" constitutes the existence of the individual soul that abides in each person and is not limited to this dimension. Psychospiritual personality development requires the ability and desire to separate, wean, and grow into a mature actualized soul.

Each soul has the potential *spiritual* energy of thousands of physical suns, provided it develops beyond the "shell consciousness" it dons while in this life. Enlightened ones all say, "Develop your self while in this crypt of the cosmos. Move away from your self-absorbed state, to union in worship of your Lord, the Absolute and Eternal." Some aspects of psychospiritual development can be compared to what Alice Bailey, author of *The Consciousness of the Atom*, called four inner stages of man.

You will have, in the early stages of human evolution, that which we might call the *atomic stage*, in which man comes to a gradual recognition that he is a self-conscious unit, with an individuality all his own. Anyone who has brought up children knows this stage well. It can be seen in the constant utterance of "my, my, my," the stage of appropriation for himself, with no thought of any other self…. Then, as life goes on, man passes out of the atomic stage to a higher and a better one, when he becomes [cognizant] of his *group relationships*…. The group consciousness begins to make itself felt…. [T]he love aspect begins to show itself…but, that there is still something greater still…. He [realizes] that he is a part of *a great universal life which underlies all groups*, he is not just a universal atom, he is not just part of a group…. The group itself has to be blended again with the consciousness of that great Identity Who is the synthesis of them all. Thus he arrives at the *final stage of intelligent appreciation of divine unity.*[92] (italics added)

Most people do not *choose* to grow beyond their group relationships, especially in regard to psychospiritual growth. The first group or community that an individual experiences is his or her family.

All the creatures on earth, and all the birds that fly with wings, are communities like you. We did not leave anything out of this book. To their Lord, all these creatures will be summoned. (6:38)

If you obey the majority of people on earth, they will divert you from the path of God. They follow only conjecture; they only guess. (6:116)

The family is the laboratory where an individual learns to interact with others. In their desire to fit into a "mainstream," many people accept conjecture presented as socially correct facts all their lives.

A person's group identities and affiliations are as varied as the person's experiences. Some groups are temporary and fleeting, while other groups have greater permanence and value. The largest group that we belong to is creation itself. Humans who use their intelligence come to understand that they are part of a greater reality that beckons them to join the rest of creation and worship the Lord of creation.

The Psychospiritual Selves

On the course to psychospiritual maturity, an individual passes through several spiritual selves. A mature person becomes capable of carrying out his or her voluntary duties as a Divinely guided human being. Some duties are specific to the individual and his or her circumstances. People's most important voluntary duties in this life are to realize that they are wholly from and dependent on God and to worship the One God. Approximately two weeks after conception, the human fetus is no larger than the period at the end of this sentence. When the molecular density of a physically mature human is compressed, the entire body's mass could easily rest on a pinhead. Bailey's example of the atom-like, small-minded self-consciousness could be considered as analogous to the external pinhead-sized physical form. The complexity of human personality extends far beyond the pinhead-sized biological body suit that expands and houses each human soul. A car cannot give rise to a driver's exhilaration after the driver reaches a desired destination; likewise, the physical form and its attachments are not keys to self-knowledge. The self must be weaned from obstinacy, selfishness, arrogance, and evil conduct. If a person rejects the Divine means of separating from negative qualities, the person is foolish and unjust to his or her self. Spiritual keys to personality development can be extracted from an understanding of the selves in *psychospiritual* growth. The psychospiritual selves blend into one another, and a person may exhibit features of several conditions and selves. Some negative psychospiritual qualities that impale the self are conceit, arrogance, confusion, estrangement, and psychic illness. Some positive qualities are insight, positive spiritual yearning, contentment, and peace.

Appetite-Driven Self (An-Nafs Al-Ammarah)

The self-centered Appetite-Driven Self (*An-Nafs Al-Ammarah*), is governed by its once pinhead-sized physical garment and its appetites. This self inclines towards sensual pleasure and satisfaction, impulsive gratification, anger, envy, greed, and conceit. Its primary concerns are preservation of the body (that is headed towards cellular decay), physical self-enhancement, and satisfaction of physical urges without regard for matters of the mind and heart. Blessings from God, the body, and its natural appetites are essential for human life. If not disciplined and regulated, lower desires stifle self-development. The scholar and poet, Jalalu'-Din Rumi, said, "If you meet someone bereft of the higher traits, be assured he is not a human being, but has put on a human form." By "human form," Rumi seems to mean that each soul is enshrouded in a human body and its appetites. Behaviors exclusive to the Appetite-Driven Self are *not* expressions of psychospiritual yearning, love, mercy, and a desire for knowledge. The Appetite-Driven Self is in Bailey's *self-absorbed* stage.

But, alas, they were totally blinded by their lust. (15:72)

Do you think that most of them hear, or understand? They are just like animals; no, they are far worse. (25:44)

God admits those who believe and lead a righteous life into gardens with flowing streams. As for those who disbelieve, they live and eat like the animals eat, then end up in the hellfire. (47:12)

Characteristics of the Appetite-Driven Self

Features of the Appetite-Driven Self are *psychospiritual faults endemic to the imperfect human nature*. A *fault is* a crack or lesion in an otherwise solid substance or structure, *something that causes inadequacy or failure*.[93] The words *imperfection* and *shortcoming* are apt descriptors of ego-based human fallibility. With Divine guidance, a healthy person learns to overcome these faults. Unbelieving souls insist that higher traits are the mere outcome of social conditioning and upbringing. In the context of the caterpillar to butterfly analogy, a person has to "eat the right foliage" in order to advance beyond the Appetite-Driven Self. Some characteristics of individuals governed by the Appetite-Driven Self are:

1. Denial; no or limited willingness to acknowledge or admit unwanted facts.

    Some would say, "Our minds are made up!" Instead, it is a curse from God, as a consequence of their disbelief, that keeps them from believing, except for a few of them. (2:88)

Denial is *rooted in fear of the truth and the exposure of blameworthy deeds*. When a person stops fleeing from the truth, he or she is able to acknowledge seemingly uncomfortable facts about life. Satan is quite effective in convincing millions of people that the truth hurts.

2. Weakness; lack of fortitude, strength, and focus to accomplish certain tasks.

Because their minds are oblivious to this, they commit works that do not conform with this; their works are evil. Then, when we requite their leaders with retribution, they complain. (23:63-64)

A weak spiritual heart paralyzes a healthy mind and body. The paralysis need not be visible to the physical eye. Weakness of the body cannot paralyze a healthy spiritual heart and mind. The spiritually fainthearted *erroneously* regard life tests intended to grow their souls as too difficult or risky. God does not overburden human beings.

3. Selfishness.

[S]elfishness is a human trait, and if you do good and lead a righteous life, God is fully Cognizant of everything you do. (4:128, partial)

This person loves his or her illusionary selfish self who eats, drinks, sleeps, accumulates, and puffs itself up. The person's thoughts center only on preserving the illusion rather than growing the real self that resides behind the fading illusion.

4. Adversarial outlook; tendency to act against or oppose valid standards of conduct.

Those who disbelieved are allies of one another. Unless you keep these commandments, there will be chaos on earth, and terrible corruption. (8:73)

Some individuals enjoy opposing revealed moral structures. By virtue of their different outer agendas, they do not appear to hold much in common with each other. However, those who oppose moral precepts are closely aligned in that they are in rebellion against Divine guidance.

5. Ingratitude; lack of appreciation.

When adversity touches the human being, he implores us while lying down, or sitting, or standing up. But as soon as we relieve his adversity, he goes on as if he never implored us to relieve any hardship! (10:12, partial)

This person feels entitled and sees no need to be grateful and appreciative to God. These individuals consider it painful to acknowledge that they need help or assistance from others, let alone a Supreme Compassionate Lord and Creator.

6. Depression, hopelessness, and disappointment when tested with strained circumstances.

   The human being never tires of imploring for good things. And when adversity befalls him, he turns despondent, desperate. (41:49)

This person wants to define the times and circumstances that amount to personal life tests and conveniently ignores how he or she has contributed to some negative situations. When a person loses sight of the true psychospiritual path, he or she frequently feels disheartened and depressed rather than resilient and hopeful.

7. Neglect, carelessness; inattentiveness to spiritual welfare; engrossed in past times of life.

   God is the One who increases the provision for whomever He wills, or withholds it. They have become preoccupied with this life, and this life, compared to the Hereafter, is nil. (13:26)

A tragedy of catastrophic proportions occurs when a person discounts the purpose of human life. The person becomes absorbed in the accumulation of power, prestige, and possessions.[94] Like someone walking towards quicksand, each step beckons disaster. In the absence of psychospiritual recovery, the quicksand of worldly preoccupation eventually swallows the person.

8. Stinginess; unwillingness to share or spend for fear of loss.

   Proclaim, "If you possessed my Lord's treasures of mercy, you would have withheld them, fearing that you might exhaust them. The human being is stingy." (17:100)

This person holds back. When he or she gives, the portions are inadequate, even when there is more than enough to share. Good portions of whatever kind may appear to originate from a good harvest or heart, but the portions actually come from God.

9. Denial of the existence of God.

They are like the devil: he says to the human being, "Disbelieve," then as soon as he disbelieves, he says, "I disown you. I fear God, Lord of the universe." (59:16)

Spiritually disturbed individuals and communities claim that people who deny the existence of God are intelligent, enlightened, and courageous thinkers. The Devil regards such humans as foolish.

10. Reluctance to take a stand for fear of not pleasing one party or another; vacillation about clear matters and following own opinions.

    The only people who wish to be excused are those who do not really believe in God and the Last Day. Their hearts are full of doubt, and their doubts cause them to waver. (9:45)

    No soul can believe except in accordance with God's will. For He places a curse upon those who refuse to understand. (10:100)

It is one thing to have doubt about an unclear matter and quite another thing to have doubt about a proven reality. Doubts about objective incontrovertible facts reflect ignorance, fear, weakness of heart, cowardice, and a need to feel beyond reproach. Before being placed in this "crypt of the cosmos," humans doubted God's Omnipotence *when in His Presence.* Unyielding doubt and following irretractable false opinions are Divine curses that beset a person who does not want to acknowledge the truth and grow his or her soul.

11. Impatience; unwillingness to see matters through to their completion; distraction from the Truth by superficial matters.

    The human being often prays for something that may hurt him, thinking that he is praying for something good. The human being is impatient. (17:11)

    O people, God's promise is the truth; therefore, do not be distracted by this lowly life. Do not be diverted from God by mere illusions. (35:5)

    Say, "I do not know if what is promised to you will happen soon, or if my Lord will delay it for awhile." (75:25)

No matter when a person wants an event or outcome to occur, the event or outcome will not occur unless it is the will of God. Oftentimes, a person insists on having or attaining something that later proves to be a source of bad fortune. A healthy person learns to be proactive, abide in the greater scheme of the creation, and be at peace with the Creator's Promise and Plan.

12. Suppression and distortion of the truth; thinking that no one is aware of his or her thoughts.

We created the human, and we know what he whispers to himself. We are closer to him than his jugular vein. (50:16)

Suppression and distortion occur when a person uses his or her reason and intellectual faculties to lie or attempt to escape a truth. Somewhere down the line, a person is convinced that such behavior effectively blocks out realities that the person is unwilling and unprepared to accept. If an individual digs deeper in his or her mind, the person discovers that the *undistorted* truths are just beneath the surface of conscious thought. Imagine placing an object in a dark corner of a basement because you do not want to think of it or be reminded of it (suppression and distortion). Eventually, you forget about it. But before you even became aware that the specific object existed, before you even thought of hiding it, someone knew that you were going to hide the object in a basement. Your unspoken thoughts may be hidden from others, but they are not hidden from The One who knows your thoughts before you even become aware of them. An unbelieving self (*nafs kafarah*) or atheist attempts to hide and supplant Divine truth.

13. Fearfulness and unease when fortunes and fate falter; tendency to worry and experience anxiety; a generalized fear about life called "existential anxiety."

Indeed, the human being is anxious. If touched by adversity, despondent. If blessed by wealth, stingy. (70:19-21)

The allegory of those who accept other masters beside God is that of the spider and her home; the flimsiest of all homes is the home of the spider, if they only knew. (29:41)

As long as a person places his or her security and success in the hands of someone or something other than God, that security and success is as fragile as a spider's web (29:41). Yet, to the person in the "spider's web," it may seem otherwise. Devoid of the knowledge that God knows and controls all things, a psychospiritually immature person is often fearful, anxious, and worried, despite presenting a facade of confidence and reassurance. The mind and body pay a heavy price for chronic real or imagined insecurity and fear.

14. Narrow-mindedness; rejection of the idea of life beyond this world.

> *They care only about things of this world that are visible to them, while being totally oblivious to the Hereafter. (30:7)*

This person wants to be seen as sober, realistic, and down-to-earth. If the person cannot see it, smell it, taste it, touch it, dissect it, monitor it, count it, or measure it, then "it" is deemed nonexistent. The person believes that there is no room for an afterlife or non-physical Reality that creates all things.

15. Excessive accumulation of or preoccupation with material possessions.

> *The human being is unappreciative of his Lord. He bears witness to this fact. He loves material things excessively. (100:6-8)*

Some individuals' self-esteem and identity largely depends on the amount and quality of their material possessions. They spend time talking about their possessions, overindulging their bodies, and are preoccupied with seeking means to obtain material things. Their souls are crushed under the weight of their love of the material.

16. Externalization and blame of others for his or her wrongdoings.

> *They will also say, "Our Lord, we have obeyed our masters and leaders, but they led us astray. (33:67)*

The blame game begins in childhood when people play it to avoid the consequences of misdeeds. Children should be taught not to fear taking responsibility for their actions so that when they become adults, they will be less likely to falsely blame others or erroneously claim that others misled them. No individual is faultless. With psychospiritual growth, a person learns that it is better to acknowledge wrongdoings.

In so doing, the soul can heal and grow. After this life, the opportunity to play the blame game is over.

Law-Abiding Self (An-Nafs Al Lawwamah)

The *Law-Abiding Self* (*Nafs Al Lawwamah*) warns a person against acting *outside* of innate and learned parameters of lawful moral behavior. Innate parameters reflect: 1) survival instincts against physical dangers and 2) an intuitive awareness of some situations and conditions that may augur psychospiritual danger. This principle is reflected in the popular saying, "The first *law* of nature is self-preservation." Parents, teachers, and others in society teach individuals the parameters or rules of life and social interaction that govern the Law-Abiding Self.

The essential feature of the Law-Abiding Self is the spiritual conscience. The spiritual conscience warns a person against internal prompts and whispers *(waswasi)* from Satan. *The conscience or Law-Abiding Self cautions a person against retaining faults of the* Appetite-Driven Self. The conscience reproaches a person for not heeding the warnings, and the reproach may engender feelings of guilt, a repentant posture, individual recommitment to ignore satanic prompts, and renewed vigor to heed God's guidance. If unlawful behavior does not engender reexamination of feelings and behavior, the person who breaks the law either lacks the cognitive capacity to understand what happened or knowingly chooses to ignore the warnings. The Law-Abiding Self does not subjugate a person with overbearing restrictions; instead, it keeps the person on guard against *domination* by lower desires and unrighteousness urges *(sha'wah)*. Humans compose overbearing suffocating restrictions.; wanting to feel superior to others, unhealthy souls find satisfaction in overburdening others with man-made restrictions. By contrast, God's commands foster psychospiritual growth.

> *Those who are blessed with knowledge will recognize the truth from your Lord, and then believe in it, and their hearts will readily accept it. Most assuredly, God guides the believers in the right path. (22:54)*

Individuals who repeatedly violate God's commands find the commands too burdensome, an affront to their individual freedom, or impossible to keep. When the Law-Abiding Self heeds its conscience, a psychospiritual door opens towards attraction to virtue and righteousness, and the person is led out of spiritual darkness into light. *The Law-Abiding Self is the first stage of psychospiritual growth.*

The Law-Abiding Self warns a person against acting *outside* of innate and learned parameters of lawful moral behavior. The Law-Abiding Self is present in Alice Bailey's *group* stage of inner human evolution. A person first learns rules of interaction in the family and identifies with family members. Then, a person learns formal and informal social mores, obeys laws, and becomes a contributing member of society. A conscientious moral person gravitates towards Divine laws and seeks to heed God's guidance. In the later phase of this stage, a person comes to realize that there is a great universal life that underlies all else in this world. The spiritual light brightens, and the self experiences inspiration to obey and please God. All subsequent stages of psychospiritual development are graduations towards the worship of God alone and self-actualization in the Divine unity.

Spiritually Inspired Self (An-Nafs Al-Mulhima)

The *Spiritually Inspired Self* (*An-Nafs Al-Mulhima*) wants to become righteous and pious, seeks spiritual truth, and resolves to please God as much as possible. Having matured beyond obedience merely to avoid punishment or accrue rewards, the Spiritually Inspired Self seeks good for its own value. This person realizes that the light of self-illumination is attained by following the Light of God. An aspirant's ambition or ideal *(himma)* is to receive and benefit from God's guidance and actively reflect on his or her actions. Instead of behaving vindictively or condescendingly towards others, the aspirant seeks to face his or her shortcomings and psychospiritual illnesses. Reflection or contemplation is characterized by being appreciative of Divine blessings and performing Divinely ordained acts of worship.

> *Say, "I am no more than a human like you, being inspired that your god is one god. Those who hope to meet their Lord shall work righteousness, and never worship any other god beside his Lord." (18:110)*

In progressing towards actualization, the positive Spiritually Inspired Self does *not* abandon parameters for righteous conduct or acts of worship. Such abandonment grows out of a person believing that he or she has advanced spiritually beyond obedience to certain Divinely revealed commands. Such abandonment reflects 1) delusions of having special knowledge not given to others, 2) the illusion that one may have been chosen as a special guide to others, and 3) a degradation of personal spiritual yearning. Inspiration also flows in an unhealthy psychospiritual direction. Individuals intent on opposing Divine guidance are inspired to embrace Satan's point of view.

> *We have permitted the enemies of every prophet—human and jinn devils—to inspire in each other fancy words, in order to deceive. Had your Lord willed, they would not have done it. You shall disregard them and their fabrications. (6:112)*

Content Self (An-Nafs Al-Qana'ah)

The *Content Self (An-Nafs Al-Qana'ah)* is satisfied with the good provisions it has, and not given to longing for what others have. The Content Self is not driven to be on equal material terms with others out of fear that any diminution in "status" reflects inferiority or failure. The Content Self does not hesitate to seek God's provisions. The Content Self is aware that dissatisfaction with God's provisions reflects ungratefulness and spiritual immaturity. Neither fatalistic nor disheartened, the Content Self views negative circumstances as opportunities to make corrections, improve his or her trust in God, and reaffirm that no individual can acquire any good unless it is the will of God. The Content Self is moderate and temperate, not prone to extreme or exorbitant behaviors (such as self-indulgence, debilitating anger, and overreaction to situations), and is aware that God knows what is best.

> *We will surely test you through some fear, hunger, and loss of money, lives, and crops. Give good news to the steadfast. (2:155)*

> *God is the One who increases the provision for whomever He chooses from among His creatures, and withholds it. God is fully aware of all things. (29:62)*

Calm Peaceful Self (An-Nafs Al-Mut'mainnah)

An extension of the Content Self, the *Calm Peaceful Self (An-Nafs Al-Mut'mainnah), exhibits composure and peace.* This person does not harbor desires for recognition from others nor is he or she anxious when in the presence of others. This Calm Peaceful Self hopes to be admitted into God's Presence after this life and finds deep satisfaction in the remembrance of God. Purified of tensions, the Calm

Peaceful Self emerges victorious in the struggle against obstacles that block the path to inner peace. The Calm Peaceful self no longer becomes unraveled by events and circumstances. Instead, what is understood by the unenlightened to be the person's "passivity" is actually righteous submission to God, not a disheartened resignation to negative circumstances.

Happy Joyful Self (An Nafs Al-Radiyah)

Another extension of the Content Self, the *Happy Joyful Self (An-Nafs Al-Radiyah)* is *happy* that God is pleased with it. *Happiness is a quality of the soul.* The Happy Joyful Self beseeches God to grant it comfort and ease in submission to Him alone. This self abhors even the slightest satanic impulse away from its nature as a creature-submitter to God. This person seeks protection in this life from evil and Satan. Recognizing that God is the Benefactor and creation is the beneficiary, the Happy Joyful Self unhesitatingly obeys the Benefactor. A fully functioning person, the Happy Joyful Self is able to carry out his or her psychospiritual duties. At the time of departure from this life, the Happy Joyful Self joins the company of its spiritual companions in Paradise. The self is at rest, reassured, and relaxed (*an-nafs murtah*). *The Happy Joyful Self is the final stage of psychospiritual personality growth in this life.*

Some faces, on that day, will be happy. (75:22)

As for you, O content soul. Return to your Lord, pleased and pleasing. Welcome into My servants. Welcome into My Paradise. (89:27-30)

Then there are those who dedicate their lives to serving God; God is compassionate towards such worshipers. (2:207)

Perfected Self (An-Nafs Al-Kalimah)

A grace and mercy of God, the spiritual perfection of the *Perfected Self (An-Nafs Al-Kalimah)* is actualization in the One True Reality. Like the droplet that reunites with the ocean from whence it came, the complete, perfected self gains *all* in losing the nothing that is disguised as popularity, prestige, and possession in this life. There are no shadowy impressions of opposition to the Absolute, no veils of the senses, no veils of a rancid ego, no veils of a corrupt intellect, no veils of absence and presence, no conceit, and no arrogance. There is only the One Reality.

Only those who come to God with their whole heart (will be saved). (26:89)

He created the heavens and the earth for a specific purpose, designed you and perfected your design, then to Him is the final destiny. (64:3)

This degree of psychospiritual development is not attained in this life. Some individuals are brought near enough to experience the gnosis that characterizes an illumined, perfecting consciousness. The perfected self dies out of any sense of existence that is independent and separate from its Lord. By God's grace, the Perfected Self is granted approach in the Divine Presence.

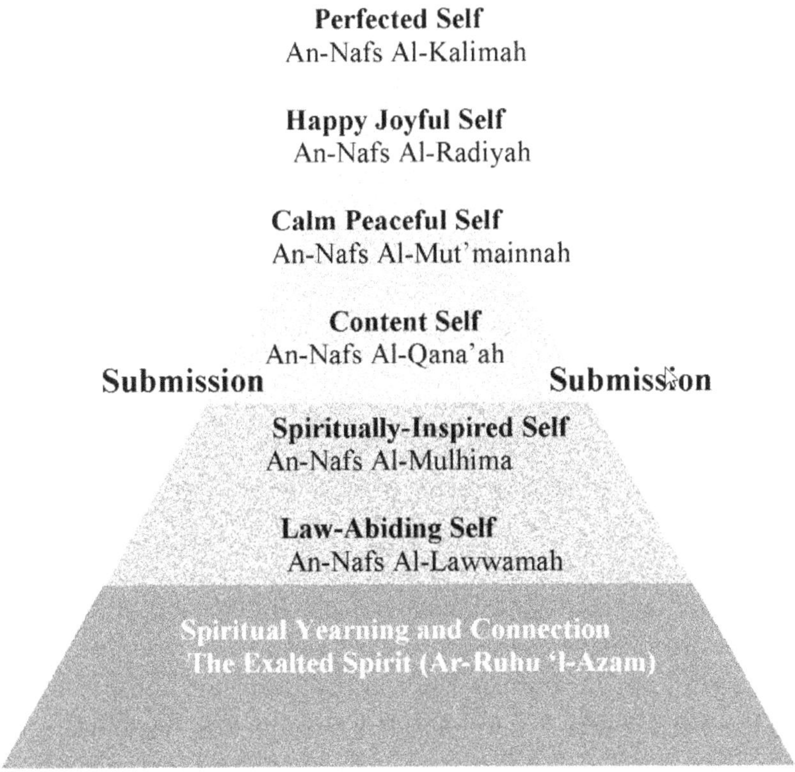

Perfected Self
An-Nafs Al-Kalimah

Happy Joyful Self
An-Nafs Al-Radiyah

Calm Peaceful Self
An-Nafs Al-Mut'mainnah

Content Self
An-Nafs Al-Qana'ah

Submission   **Submission**

Spiritually-Inspired Self
An-Nafs Al-Mulhima

Law-Abiding Self
An-Nafs Al-Lawwamah

**Spiritual Yearning and Connection
The Exalted Spirit (Ar-Ruhu 'l-Azam)**

Figure 5.2 Hierarchy of Psychospiritual Development.

The Law-Abiding Self (Figure 4.1) learns to cooperate and abide by cultural and social prescriptions of appropriate behavior. If inspired to seek God's Pleasure, a person inclines towards righteousness for its own sake. Spiritually comatose, the Appetite-Driven Self is not depicted on this psychospiritual hierarchy.

Submission Made Difficult

Some individuals have placed on themselves (or have had placed on them by others) exorbitant expectations and pressures regarding the "acceptability" of their worship practices and spiritual steadfastness. The Creator does not overburden human beings or condemn sincere but psychospiritually immature individuals for their failings. Humans are spiritually immature and prone to compromise the worship of God alone. Were that not the case, humanity would be in the Presence of God. If humans were called to task in this life for their sins and mistakes, the earth would be lifeless.

> God never burdens a soul beyond its means: to its credit is what it earns, and against it is what it commits. "Our Lord, do not condemn us if we forget or make mistakes. Our Lord, and protect us from blaspheming against You, like those before us have done. Our Lord, protect us from sinning until it becomes too late for us to repent. Pardon us and forgive us. You are our Lord and Master. Grant us victory over the disbelieving people" (2:86).

> If God punished the people for their transgressions, He would have annihilated every creature on earth. But He respites them for a specific, predetermined time. Once their interim ends, they cannot delay it by one hour, nor advance it. (16:61)

Some individuals tend to place litmus tests, extra duties, and so-called obligatory practices never ordained by God on themselves and others. As a result, some people are pushed away from cultivating their spiritual yearning. Some learn to ape or repeat by rote what others in their religious communities say and do. Scared to make a mistake and feel inadequate, some withdraw altogether from expressing their thoughts and performing their religious practices when around individuals who constantly "correct" (actually criticize and condemn) them.

Refrain from blocking every path, seeking to repel those who believe from the path of God, and do not make it crooked. Remember that you used to be few and He multiplied your number. Recall the consequences for the wicked. (7:86)

There are countless real scenarios of harsh, demanding parents requiring perfection from their children or constantly ridiculing them, of teachers humiliating students, supervisors intimidating employees, spouses scorning and rejecting their partners, and so on. The message is always, "You cannot or did not make the grade or meet up to my expectations. You do not deserve my approval."

I recall two cases from three decades ago that vividly demonstrate the impact attempting to meet excessive and harsh religious expectations can have on a person's mental stability. In the first case, a young woman who had recently joined a small religious community was in the habit of taking her child on the commuter train each week to attend prayers. When completing the pre-prayer ritual washing, some women repeatedly told her that she did not wipe completely or she wiped specific areas too few or too many times. The woman's fears and anxiety about not correctly completing the washing escalated with each obligatory Friday visit to the mosque. Nevertheless, she wanted to fulfill her duty to God and attend prayer. One Friday, while riding the commuter train with her child, the woman lapsed into an anxiety-induced catatonic state. She became immobile, fell into a stupor, and did not respond to any verbal communication. Concerned passengers and commuter train officials comforted the woman's child. After undergoing an emergency psychiatric evaluation, the unresponsive woman was taken to a community house where fellow members of her religious community attended to her. The women at the house were instructed to tell the woman that God loved her each time they brought her meals. Several days later, after receiving a meal, the trembling woman moved towards her room door and slowly opened it. At that time, others in the house immediately came to her door, embraced her, and reassured her that God loved her and that they also loved her. In tears, the recovered woman thanked God, accepted their embraces, and asked to see her child.

In another case, an intelligent young man learned Arabic, immersed himself in reams of Muslim literature and scholarly papers, and memorized many verses from the Quran. The young man took no reprieve from his compulsive religious studies. He was highly regarded in his community and seemed to be the epitome of the community's perception of an ideal, sincere Muslim. While symbolically stoning Satan during his Hajj pilgrimage to Mecca, the young man experienced a psychotic break and was taken to the Hospital. Upon returning to the States, the man temporarily resided in the basement of a house, where it was reported that he defecated on himself, used profanity, made vocalizations as if he were a demon, threatened others, and assumed animal-like postures and behavior. The young man was clearly psychotic (i.e., possessed, *majnun*). Despite his knowledge of scripture, attention to religious ritual, and incessant religious practice, he succumbed to whispers or suggestions (*waswasi*) from Satan while performing the symbolic stoning. By God's grace, the young man was released from the psychotic state when invocations from the Quran were made to God and Quran verses were read to remove the demons (*jinn*) from the young man's mind.

Neither the young woman nor the young man in these cases suffered from organic nervous conditions that precipitated their reactions. They did not have a history of any previous psychiatric disorders or mental health problems. Both individuals were apparently overwhelmed and flooded with terrifying fears and thoughts of personal inadequacy. In the case of the young woman, her thoughts were never hidden. In the case of the young man, his surface persona and laudable religious practice masked chronic fear and feelings that he was not knowledgeable enough and strong enough to resist Satan's whispers. There are hundreds of individuals from different religions who have had similar experiences varying in severity. In such cases, a common thread is self-imposed or external pressure (masked as God's commands) to perform up to others' expectations and requirements. Individuals should ask no more of themselves than what God enjoins on them; only God knows a person's innermost intentions.

And God knows whatever you conceal and whatever you declare. (16:19)

Your Lord is fully aware of your innermost thoughts. If you maintain righteousness, He is Forgiver of those who repent. (17:25)

The common thread in the relief of these stressful symptoms was the victims' awareness and reassurance of God's Mercy. Under certain conditions and circumstances, individuals who may genuinely seek to please God experience discomfort. As illustrated by the experience of Job, confidence in God is the key to overcoming such situations. Moses' frightened mother found reassurance that her infant was safe. Although Satan encourages us to do otherwise, we should always seek ultimate assurance from our Creator and take solace that our Creator overlooks our unintentional mistakes and misdeeds. This is the bedrock of a secure mind.

And Job implored his Lord: "Adversity has befallen me, and, of all the merciful ones, You are the Most Merciful." (21:83)

The mind of Moses' mother was growing so anxious that she almost gave away his identity. But we strengthened her heart, to make her a believer…. Thus, we restored him to his mother, in order to please her, remove her worries, and to let her know that God's promise is the truth. However, most of them do not know. (28:10, 13)

"Our Lord, let not our hearts waver, now that You have guided us. Shower us with Your mercy; You are the Grantor." (3:8)

Some people think that hardships and suffering are an index of spiritual strength or a pious personality. Not so. God has made the sincere to love faith and truth, and they find no discomfort in seeking it. True comfort is found in embracing the real self that loves God. The sincere do not invite difficulty on themselves or attempt to place extra burdens and rules that God never ordained. Regarding Satan's influence on sincere worshippers, God told Satan that Satan has no power over His sincere worshippers.

"You have no power over My servants. You only have power over the strayers who follow you." (15:42)

God commands humans to seek His guidance and provision. Reluctance to implore God emanates from Satan. The more spiritually mature a person is, the more the person recognizes that God should be beseeched for guidance. Guided souls do not experience excessive despair, and they recognize that chronic despair reflects doubt about God's Omnipotence and Mercy.

Healthy Consciousness Matures into God-Consciousness

As the self grows and matriculates through the psychospiritual stages, the self evolves toward unsullied God-consciousness and connection to the True Reality. If the self is a victim of *arrested psychospiritual development*, growth does not occur.

Growth in psychospiritual consciousness may be likened to being wet. Imagine that "wetness" is a miniscule degree of higher consciousness. An inspired person experiences being wet as positive and seeks to be "drenched" in water. Like a drop of water, the person traverses through many stages and conditions. The drop eventually reunites and is engulfed in the water source from whence it emerged. In contrast to a person who experiences being wet as positive, another person attempts to be as dry as possible. A "dry" person can never attain the contact and absorption (God-consciousness) that a "wet" person attains.

The entire creation, from the smallest subatomic particle to the largest dimension of creation, is God-conscious. Animate or inanimate, each creature expresses God-consciousness in the manner consistent with its nature and purpose. This is God's system.

You do not get into any situation, nor do you recite any Quran, nor do you do anything, without us being witnesses thereof as you do it. Not even an atom's weight is out of your Lord's control, be it in the heavens or the earth. Nor is there anything smaller than an atom, or larger that is not recorded in a profound record. (10:61)

VI

Self-Effacement

Ego: Enemy of Authentic Self

At first glance, self-effacement may seem to clash with self-development and self-preservation. From a psychospiritual perspective, effacement (*afaa*) means to wipe out or eliminate something *in order to be restored to health*. To restore someone to health, efforts must be taken to eliminate any toxins, illness, or disease. The toxic "I" (i.e., ego) contends with the innate yearning for the Exalted Spirit. Fearing effacement,[95] the toxic *I* places greater importance on polishing, shining, and displaying its physical carriage. The ego wants to be recognized and heard. If it could speak, the ego would declare:

> "Whatever *I* am doing that *I* deem admirable, *I* want others to know that *I* am doing it. *I* search for suggestions and means to improve my image and negotiate with the eyes that see me. What they see about me should make them like, envy, and respect me. If they do not know what to recognize or give me credit for, *I* help them by telling them who *I* am, possibly where *I* am from, and all the outstanding things *I* have done, *I* am doing, and plan to do. *I* feel best when people realize that *I* should not be ignored or dismissed. While *I* will not violate certain rules and make things difficult for myself, *I* satisfy my urges in any manner that pleases me."

Thus, the Divine command to *kill your ego*:

> *[Y]ou shall kill your egos. This is better for you in the sight of your Creator. He did redeem you. He is the Redeemer, Most Merciful. (2:54, partial)*

Have you noted the one whose god is his ego? Consequently, God sends him astray, despite his knowledge, seals his hearing and his mind, and places a veil on his eyes. Who then can guide him, after such a decision by God? Would you not take heed? (45:23)

For individuals governed by their egos, self-effacement is tantamount to self-annihilation, but for our own good, the Creator warns us to rid ourselves of ego. The real self does not fear annihilation. *Each individual has been conditioned to believe that the false evil self (ego) is the real self.* Self-centeredness (*hubb' ad-dhat*) or egotism increases as the desire for the allurements of life exceeds healthy boundaries. Self-centered individuals believe that the satisfaction of their own desires supersedes acknowledging the needs and desires of others. In contrast to this ego-driven self-centeredness, genuine self-actualization is attained in love of God, the love that envelops a sincere seeker's soul. Our Creator grants love for Him to those who yearn for Him. In the absence of spiritual yearning, self-respect, self-esteem, and self-confidence are mere vanities. Unlike Freud's good "ego," the same ego is described in psychospiritual language as self-centered and indulgent, rationalizing violations of Divine guidance and deviating from its inborn nature to submit to God. The ego falls into disuse when a person activates his or her spiritual yearning and consciously connects with the existence of God. Recall that the compressed physical mass of a human being can easily rest on top of a pinhead. The human "dot" is not an independent entity. If *I* (a dot) think that reality is whatever *I* define it as, *I* am far adrift from my innate psychospiritual nature. God grants self-consciousness to each soul so that each soul can remember and bear witness to its Lord.

Everyone on earth perishes. Only the presence of your Lord lasts. Possessor of Majesty and Honor. (55: 26-27)

Did the human being forget that we created him already, and he was nothing? (19:67)

Genuine self-effacement is synonymous with willful submission to God. If this is too difficult for a person to grasp, the person has not yet realized that his or her sense of self (i.e., the sense of existing and being conscious) is not self-generated. A true Submitter self-effaces by witnessing that there is no deity but the One God. Effacement *is* self-knowledge (*ma'rifat un-nafs*). When the Creator manifests His

Glory or grants an individual a glimpse of what is beyond this sensory-bound consciousness, the false self that the individual thinks so highly, ceases to exist.

To your Lord is the ultimate destiny. (96: 8)

Prophet Moses experienced self-effacement when he asked to "see" God. God called upon Moses to look at a mountaintop, then God made manifest what He willed of His Glory. The mountaintop crumbled.

[He] said, "My Lord, let me look and see You." He said, "You cannot see Me. Look at that mountain; if it stays in its place, then you can see Me." Then, his Lord manifested Himself to the mountain, and this caused it to crumble. Moses fell unconscious. When he came to, he said, "Be You glorified. I repent to You, and I am the most convinced believer." (7: 143, partial)

In glorifying and worshipping God, the self is presented to itself as it really is: unapparent, unperceived, unrevealed, unknown, unconscious, unheedful, unenlightened, and ungrateful were it not the Will and Mercy of God to grant the soul loftier qualities. Sheik al-Junayd pointed out that:

The stage of giving up freedom of choice and action is the stage of annihilation, while the second stage where the mystic freely acts, because his will follows the will of God, is the state of abiding in God. *It is the shedding of the mortal self for the eternal, material for the spiritual, human for the divine.* The mystic at this stage is the perfect servant.[96] (italics added)

A Submitter Personality is intelligent, reflective, and responsible; has inner strength; is capable of psychospiritual growth; accepts proper guidance; is illumined, content, repentant, and at peace; glorifies and praises God; yearns to return to God; toils and travels from stage to stage; and remembers God.

The false illusionary self is lost, misguided, ignorant, confused, intoxicated with this life, blind, estranged, insane, self-possessed, separated and split, and its own enemy. It desires glory and power; is an evildoer; is conceited and arrogant; denies and mocks Truth; forgets its own nature; lacks reason; and is impatient and focused on ego-preservation. The worst of creatures, it is oppressed, oppressive, and unheedful, and tries to avoid God.

Is one who is a believer the same as one who is wicked? They are not equal. (32:18)

Are those enlightened by their Lord the same as those whose evil works are adorned in their eyes, and they follow their own opinions? (47:14)

Some individuals are not spiritually lost or intoxicated with life. They have not yet taken a stand *in this world* either to satisfy their spiritual yearnings or to tread the course of spiritual darkness. God is aware of each soul's decision prior to the soul's birth in this world. It is each individual's God-given right to choose to heed God's guidance and ego-efface or to go astray. The ego's stance *against* submission to God is a kind of self-harm and psychospiritual ruin that has no parallel in life. Conversely, the Peace from self-realization in submission to God is a lofty state that has no parallel in this life.

Those who submit completely (yus'lim waj'ha) to God, while leading a righteous life, have gotten hold of the strongest bond. For God is in full control of all things. (31:22)

The word *waj'ha* (verse 31:22) means "face, inner being, personality, essence, and the whole inner self." God knows all souls. The self cannot *consciously* submit to God without His permission. A ninth century scholar of esoteric knowledge (*ma-arifat*) of the self, Sheik Abu-Qasim al-Junayd said:

Know that you are your own veil which conceals yourself from you. Know that you cannot reach God through yourself, but that you reach Him through Him. The reason is that when God vouchsafes the vision of reaching Him, he calls upon you to seek after Him and so you do…. Thus, it is for your own sake that God protects you from yourself ….[97]

Despite being pure forms, humans ignore their true nature and become engrossed in a collection of selves born of physical sensations and trained thoughts. Not only is there nothing amiss about attending to physical and mental needs, states, and conditions, humans would perish if they ignored them. The body and mind are designed to tolerate only so much neglect before communicating to an individual that something is wrong. Being attentive and being engrossed are not the same. Unlike attentiveness, to become engrossed is to become preoccupied or excessively concerned with something to the extent that a person neglects other matters. A thought or activity that serves a beneficial purpose ceases to serve that purpose when an individual becomes overly absorbed in it. The word *nafs* means "self, person, human being, soul, and spirit."[98] In this volume, the letters (in English) of the word *nafs* signify **Neurotic Attachment to False Structures**. Put another way, in the absence of psychospiritual growth, an individual is highly prone to exhibiting irrational and excessive concern for transitory appetites, conditions, and relationships. In his book, *The Science of Religion,* Yogi Paramahansa Yogananda wrote:

> Now, being blessed and reflected spiritual Selves, why is it that we are utterly unmindful of our blissful state and are instead subject to physical and mental pain and suffering? The answer is that the spiritual self has brought on itself this present state (by whatever process it may be) by identifying itself with a transitory bodily vehicle and a restless mind. The spiritual Self, being thus identified, feels itself sorry for or delighted at a corresponding unhealthy and unpleasant or healthy and pleasant state of the body and mind. Because of this identification, the spiritual Self is being continually disturbed by their transitory states.[99]

> *Those who are not expecting to meet us, and are preoccupied with this worldly life, and are content with it, and refuse to heed our proofs; (10:7)*

> *Do not be like those who forgot God, so He made them forget themselves. These are the wicked. (59:19)*

Personality Reflects Spiritual Yearning

Some psychospiritual traits reflect the degree and quality of an individual's spiritual yearning. Using the analogy of star constellations, traits combine to form either shining positive characteristics or to form negative characteristics like dead star systems. A self-effacing Submitter gravitates towards praiseworthy qualities that please God. The obstinate conceited soul gravitates toward blameworthy qualities. Light yearns for light. Darkness yearns for darkness. Each soul is characterized by a mixture of light and darkness. Enlightened souls yearn for the Light of all things. Impoverished souls ignore their yearning and dread the Light. Referring to some of his psychiatric patients, Dr. Carl Jung said,

It is safe to say that every one of them (35 years of age or older) fell ill because he had lost that which the living religions of every age have given to their followers, and none of them have been really healed who did not regain his spiritual outlook.[100]

Self-examination (*mushahada*) should be undertaken according to God's instructions. The spiritual heart (*al-qalb ur-ruhi*) is enlivened through annihilation of the false self and its idols. The idols of the false self must be dismantled piece by piece, so that the real self can recognize and recover from psychospiritual illness. As an inspired person travels in this life, he or she beseeches the Creator for forgiveness and healing.

Therefore, be patient, for God's promise is true, and ask forgiveness for your sins, and glorify and praise your Lord night and day. (40:55)

You shall know that: "There is no other god beside God," and ask forgiveness of your sins and the sins of all believing men and women. God is fully aware of your decisions and your ultimate destiny. (47:19)

VII

The Unbelieving Self: A Spiritual Psychopath

Pattern of Estrangement and Destruction

In contemporary popular culture, the meanings of *normal* and *abnormal* have been completely blurred. When they describe behavior, individuals who use the terms *good*, *evil*, *normal*, and *abnormal* are often labeled as imposing their values on others. Some mental health professionals and social scientists have crafted and promoted an irreligious concept of personality that tolerates beliefs and behaviors deemed sinful in revealed scriptures. Today, in the absence of a universally accepted moral criterion, it seems that only the most horrendous acts and crimes are regarded as "evil." In exceptional cases, a person who commits a horrendous crime may not have the mental capacity to understand the nature of his or her criminal act. In non-exceptional cases, some pundits argue that the perpetrators of highly aberrant conduct are "mentally ill," "under severe emotional strain," and "not responsible for their acts," And as a result, such persons should not be held accountable for their actions. Instead, these pundits insist that the perpetrators need psychiatric care and treatment. Believing that there is no literal good or evil, some individuals insist that morality and normality are man-made constructs subject to modification with changing times and prevailing mores.

The clearest explanation of what constitutes good and evil and normal and abnormal behavior is in Divine revelation. Given that order and design exist throughout creation, any force or phenomenon that *violates* order and design in a manner incongruent with God's system can be construed as "unlawful," "evil," or "wrong." Perceived chaos that occurs as *a natural process* of growth and motion is ordered and lawful. The planets and heavenly bodies were once thought to move chaotically and randomly in space until man discovered laws of elliptical orbital motion and the intricate gravitational balance between celestial objects. Despite innumerable proofs of design, symmetry, and order in creation, some individuals insist that there is no Intelligent Designer or Creator. Their *deluded subjectivity* obscures evidence of the Supreme Designer (*Al-Musawwir*) and is at the heart of psychospiritual pathology.

> *Thus, He completed the seven universes in two days, and set up the laws for every universe. And we adorned the lowest universe with lamps, and placed guards around it. Such is the design of the Almighty, the Omniscient. (41:12)*

> *He is the One God; the Creator, the Initiator, the Designer (Al-Musawwir). To Him belong the most beautiful names. Glorifying Him is everything in the heavens and the earth. He is the Almighty, Most Wise. (59:24)*

> *We created man in the best design (ah'sani taq'weem). (95:4)*

One name or attribute of the Creator is *Al-Musawwir, The Supreme Designer or Supreme Architect.* The human being was created in the best design. The word *taq'weem* means "design, appraisal, blueprint, or layout." Human beings are not the latest manifestations of a lesser design yet to be fully developed or made "best" (*ah'sani*). The design of the human did not have to later be corrected or upgraded. The Creator designed and fitted humans to consciously and willfully acknowledge the One who brought them into existence. All humans are as one human being.

> *He designed you, and designed you well. He is the One who provides you with good provisions. Such is God your Lord; Most Exalted is God, Lord of the universe. (40:64, partial)*

> *He created the heavens and the earth for a specific purpose, designed you and perfected your design, then to Him is the final destiny. (64:3)*

> *He initiated you from one person, and decided your path, as well as your final destiny. We thus clarify the revelations for people who understand. (6:98)*

> *Guide us in the right path (sirat al-mustaqeem); the path of those whom You blessed; not of those who have deserved wrath, nor of the strayers. (1:6-7)*

The special fitting (i.e., psychospiritual attributes particular to the human being) includes intellect, higher consciousness, and an intuitive awareness of a Supreme Being. From God's Exalted Spirit precede the human intellect, reason, and higher consciousness. This special fitting, design, and awareness are a portion of the Creator's good provision to humans.

When a person acts according to the best design in the human nature, the person willingly acknowledges the Creator, and lives his or her life accordingly. The person's life can be generally described as upright, in harmony with a sound human nature, correct, and good. In daily prayer, Submitter Personalities beseech God, the Supreme Designer (*Al-Musawwir*), to guide them on the "right path" (*sirat al - mus'taqeem*), i.e., to enable them to lead their lives according to the best design (*taq'weem*). *This constitutes lawful, healthy, moral behavior.*

The Self that Violates the Best Design

When I initially wrote this chapter, I beseeched God Almighty, if He willed, to show me a way to illustrate how a person loses psychospiritual balance, strays from the best design, becomes psychospiritually ill, and engages in evil actions. I began to draw lines on a blank piece of paper. The picture in Figure 6.1 is the picture that I thought *I* drew. I had no idea of the hidden patterns in the picture. I exaggerated the dot in the middle of the profile to symbolize the core or heart of the psyche. As I moved the pencil, I did not want to draw circles. I spiked the lines at random points to emphasize the idea of further deviation from an already estranged pattern. I drew the broken lines in order to illustrate the idea of a person moving away from Reality into an illusionary "reality" with its own structure. After accidentally dropping the piece of paper and picking it up, patterns in the drawing that clearly show how a person loses psychospiritual balance emerged. I did not consciously draw the patterns. *All Praise be to God. God is doing everything.*

Slowly rotate Figure 7.1 clockwise. A silhouette of a small, spinning head becomes apparent. The spinning head is analogous to psychospiritual estrangement (*dalal*) and confusion. The thwarting and numbing of spiritual yearning eventually lead to estrangement and confusion. An element of a psychospiritually toxic belief or behavior is first introduced in a disguised fashion. A person is influenced and encouraged to accept it. Once one element is accepted, additional elements are presented until a person embraces all elements of a toxic belief or behavior. The person is *systematically desensitized* to 1) become comfortable with and accept evil actions and 2) dismiss warnings from his or her conscience against the actions.

Say, "Shall we implore, beside God, what possesses no power to benefit us or hurt us, and turn back on our heels after God has guided us? In that case, we would join those possessed by the devils, and rendered utterly confused, while their friends try to save them: 'Stay with us on the right path.'" Say, "God's guidance is the right guidance. We are commanded to submit to the Lord of the universe." (6:71)

O you who believe, you shall embrace total submission; do not follow the steps of Satan, for he is your most ardent enemy (lakum aduwu mubeen). (2:208)

O children of Adam, do not let the devil dupe you as he did when he caused the eviction of your parents from Paradise, and the removal of their garments to expose their bodies. He and his tribe see you, while you do not see them. We appoint the devils as companions of those who do not believe. (7:27)

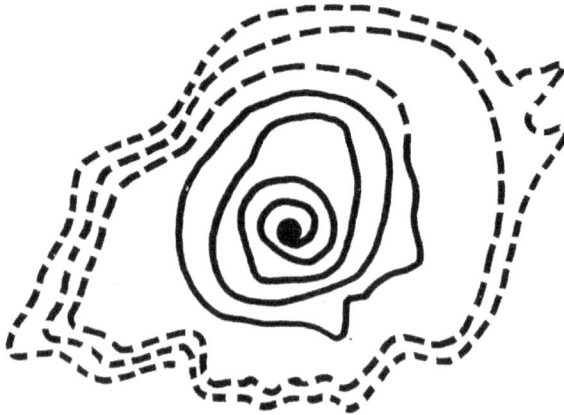

Figure 7.1. Spinning Head

By rotating Figure 7.1 counter-clockwise, a silhouette of a horned devil *(shaetan)* in broken lines becomes apparent. In drawings, broken lines may indicate something that is hidden from view or abiding in an unseen dimension. The *hidden ardent enemy (lakum aduwu mubeen)* of humans, Satan whispers *(was'wasi)* evil into the hearts (minds) of humans to divert them from 1) submission to God alone, 2) their innate best design, and 3) self-knowledge. When completely upside down (*maqlub*), the *inverted* head represents a person who is spiritually psychotic. Twelve centuries ago, Sheik al-Din Suhrawardi opined that departed individuals whose souls are darkened by evil deeds and opposition to God enter *a dark world of inverted forms*:

> On the contrary, those whose soul has been tarnished by the darkness of evil and ignorance (ashdb al-shagawah) depart for the *world of inverted forms (suwar mu'allagah)* which lies in the labyrinth of fantasy, *the dark world of the devils and the jinn.*[101] (italics added)

The drawing corroborates Suhrawardi's belief about the fate of souls engulfed in evil. Their psychospiritual illness in this life is followed in the Hereafter by spiritual habitation in Hell, the inverted "dark world of devils and jinn." Hell is separation from the Light of God and its Beautific reflections.

Indeed, those who earn sins and become surrounded by their evil work will be the dwellers of Hell; they abide in it forever. (2:81)

As for those who earned sins, their requital is equivalent to their sin. Humiliation is their lot, and no one beside God can protect them. Their faces will seem overwhelmed by masses of dark night. They will be the dwellers of Hell; they abide therein forever. (10:27)

Repentance is acceptable by God from those who fall in sin out of ignorance, then repent immediately thereafter. God redeems them. God is Omniscient, Most Wise. (4:17)

The ignorance Suhrawardi wrote about is the result of a lack of knowledge about good and evil. It is a self-imposed ignorance that characterizes souls that *refuse God's guidance.* Such refusal is the antithesis of psychospiritual personality development. Psychospiritual imbalance leads to chronic adjustment problems and varying degrees of neurosis and psychosis. A person may be spiritually psychotic (*junun*) yet appear to others as normal.[102] The rotation of the small head inside the "invisible devil" profile represents how negative (evil) thoughts invade the mind with increasing frequency, producing psychospiritual illness. The word *demented* means "mad" or "crazy." Its Latin root, *demens*, means "out of one's mind." The inverted spinning head in the drawing clearly represents a condition wherein someone is confused and out of his or her rational, balanced mind. Similar in sound and spelling to *demens*, the word *demon* means "evil spirit or devil" (*jinn*). A resolutely unbelieving self is a psychopath (*nafs marid*); the spiritual core (soul) of the psyche is diseased (*marid*). Psychopaths are typically thought of as patients in psychiatric hospitals and heartless habitual criminals, yet willful unrelenting opposition to God and His guidance is a form of psychopathy that is spiritually fatal to the obstinate opposer. Splintered from the Reality that created him or her in the "best design," the obstinate person loses psychospiritual bearings. In contrast, when the picture in Figure 6.1 is rotated clockwise, the head returns to the upright position and the devil profile is upside down, symbolic of its natural position in opposition to Absolute Peace and Order.

> *As for those who harbored doubts (maradun – diseases) in their hearts, it actually added unholiness to their unholiness, and they died as disbelievers (9:125)*

Belief in The Unseen (*al-Ghi'eeb*) is a *corequisite* to undertaking and completing the journey to becoming a Submitter Personality. The unseen spiritual realm is partly comprised of angels,[103] *jinn* beings, an eternal afterlife, spiritual accounting (i.e., the Day of Judgment) and ranking corresponding to i.e., grades of Heaven or Hell) of each soul based on the soul's level of submission to God during this life. Belief in the Unseen is a *prerequisite* for adequately understanding that a human being enters an inner inverted dark world inhabited by demons and evil jinn (as depicted in the inverted human head inside the devil profile). *Jinn* are fallen angels and the offspring of Satan.

> The other half of the guilty creatures, [the first half are humans] those who leaned closer to Satan's point of view and exhibited the biggest egos, became classified as jinns. It was God's plan to assign one jinn to every human being from birth to death. The jinn companion represents Satan and constantly promotes his point of view (50:23, 27)…Both the jinns and the humans are given a precious chance in this world to re-educate themselves, denounce their egoism, and redeem themselves by submitting to God's absolute authority. Whenever a human is born, a jinn is born and is assigned to the new human. We learn from the Quran that the jinns are Satan's descendents (7:27, 18:50)…the jinn remains a constant companion of the human until the human dies. The jinn is freed and lives on for a few centuries. Both jinns and humans are required [but not forced] to worship God alone. (51:56)[104]

The [jinn] companion said, "Here is my formidable testimony"…His [jinn] companion said, "Our Lord, I did not mislead him; he [this human] was far astray." (50:23, 27)

O children of Adam, do not let the devil dupe you as he did when he caused the eviction of your parents from Paradise, and the removal of their garments to expose their bodies. He and his tribe see you, while you do not see them. We appoint the devils as companions of those who do not believe. (7:27)

We said to the angels, "Fall prostrate before Adam." They fell prostrate, except Satan. He became jinn, for he disobeyed the order of His Lord. Will you choose him and his descendants as lords instead of Me, even though they are your enemies? What a miserable substitute! (18:50)

In this cosmic crypt, jinn need more time to study God's signs. Unlike humans, jinn *were not* given instinctive knowledge that God alone is the Lord and Master, though they receive and hear the same Divine revelations given to humans. God invested jinn with abilities to study His signs in realms throughout this universe that are imperceptible and inaccessible to humans. If a person sincerely embraces God's guidance, the person's jinn companion is eventually convinced and submits to God.

Say, "I was inspired that a group of jinns listened, then said, We have heard a wonderful Quran. "It guides to righteousness, and we have believed in it; we will never set up any idols besides our Lord. "The Most High is our only Lord. He never had a mate, nor a son. (72:1-3)

The movement of the human profile away from its upright position (i.e., psychospiritual health) reflects the influence or strength of attraction *(ijtizaab)* of the jinn's message to violate God's commands and guidance. A soul meanders from the upright to the nearly-inverted positions until it gains enough spiritual strength to dismiss most of the jinn's messages. Submitter Personalities invoke the name of God and seek refuge when taunted by suggestions from Satan's internal representative.

When the devil whispers (was'wasi) to you any whisper, seek refuge in God; He is Hearer, Omniscient. (7:200)

Similar to *majnun*, the word *majzub* means possessed, mentally ill, or insane. The term *majzub* also indicates that the specific mental illness or possession results from heeding suggestions from Satan's internal representative, the jinn. Majzub is induced in a person when the person *is attracted and succumbs to enticements and influences (ijtizaab) presented by an internal "enticer" or the enticer's human agents. Majzub denotes illness in the innermost realm (i.e., soul) of the psyche or consciousness.* Many mental illnesses are not brought about by knowingly embracing satanic suggestions, nor are the illnesses brought on by corruption of the psychospiritual core of consciousness. Souls or personalities that become majzub are farthest removed from the Light of God and enveloped by a devil enticer. Dr. Carl Jung captured some characteristics of psychospiritual pathos in the concept he defined as the *shadow*:

> By shadow, I mean the negative side of personality, the sum of all the unpleasant qualities.[105]

In his book, *Without Conscience*, Dr. Robert Hare cited the description of a psychopath forwarded by Robert Linder. According to Linder,

> The psychopath is a rebel, a religious disobeyer of prevailing codes and standards… a rebel without a cause, an agitator without a slogan, and a revolutionary without a program; in other words, his rebelliousness is aimed to achieve goals satisfactory to him alone; he is incapable of exertions for the sake of others. All his efforts, under no matter what guise, represent investments designed to satisfy his immediate wishes and desires.[106]

Linder's description presents a psychopath as self-centered and in rebellion against *all* rules and authority. In contrast, a psychospiritual psychopath does *not* rebel against all rules and authority. The psychospiritual psychopath embraces rules of his or her own making or someone else's making, *as long as the rules do not bind to or remind the psychospiritual psychopath of any moral or spiritual responsibilities.* The psychospiritual psychopath has a cause—hatred of the Highest Authority (God). This type of psychopath often disguises this hatred as "intelligent, mature thinking," "being self-assured," and "being anchored in the real world."

In the nineteenth century, the idea of "moral insanity" emerged, but it did not receive acceptance beyond the religious communities that introduced it. A reverend and writer in the nineteenth century, Charles G. Finney said:

Moral insanity, on the other hand, is will-madness. The man retains his intellectual powers unimpaired, but he sets his heart fully to evil. He refuses to yield on the demands of his conscience. He practically discards the obligations of moral responsibility. He has the powers of free moral agency, but persistently abuses them. He has a reason which affirms obligation, but he refuses obedience to its affirmations…. In this form of insanity, the reason remains unimpaired; but the heart deliberately disobeys…. The insanity spoken of in the text is moral, that of the heart. By the heart here, is meant the will—the voluntary power. While the man is intellectually sane, he yet acts as if he were intellectually insane…. Every man knows that insane people actually follow the wild dreams of their own fancy, as if they were the most stern reality and can scarcely be made to feel the force of anything truly real…. So men, in their sins, treat the realities of the spiritual world as if they were not real, but follow the most empty phantoms of this world, as if they were stern realities….[107]

In the early twentieth century, moral insanity was defined as insanity of the moral system, "badness alleged to be irresponsible."[108] The phrase "badness alleged to be irresponsible" means that certain evil actions (i.e., badness) were reframed as mere socially irresponsible behavior or poor judgment.

Theophobia and Theophobic Personality Disorder

The resolute unbelieving self is *majzub* and a *Theophobe*. The word, *phobic*, means morbid fear or aversion. *Theo* means "God." (In this case, a small *t* is inappropriate because the term, Theophobe, refers specifically to fear or denial of the Supreme Being.) Psychological suppression involves *consciously* pushing back unacceptable thoughts and striving to keep what is unacceptable out of awareness. In cases of *Theophobia*, God-consciousness, moral principles and values, and a sense of Divinely rooted moral responsibility and accountability are unacceptable thoughts. Theophobes make every effort to free themselves from positive thoughts about religion and God. Their "morality" is solely derived from social ethics, wholly secular expositions of appropriate and inappropriate behavior, and their personal opinions.

The terms, *Theophobe* and *Theophobia*, are not in the dictionary or psychiatric manuals delineating mental disorders. In Western society, a chasm traditionally exists between psychological health as defined in the mental health professions and Divinely rooted themes of psychological health. It is unlikely that the mental health professions will adopt the terms, *Theophobe* and *Theophobia* (or similar terms) in the near future. Some individuals have attempted to divest mental health annals and dialogue of any mention of God, spirituality, or religion. Other mental health students and professionals have incorporated spiritual themes by requesting their clients to indicate if religion or spirituality is important to them. Mirroring a recent growing interest in spiritual themes in the larger society, many mental health professionals are increasingly interested in the impact of spirituality on personality and mental health. Some professionals are incorporating spiritual themes in their interactions with their clients. More students in training for mental health careers are expressing interest in the relationship between spirituality and mental health. Yet, this trend should not be interpreted as an index of the extent that mental health students and professionals are exhibiting *personal* interest in psychospiritual development.

Modern psychiatry and psychology do not recognize or have a formal diagnostic classification for the symptoms and features of Theophobia. *Nevertheless, a chronic irretractable aversion towards God and spiritual themes is a serious mental illness.* Each individual chooses to become afflicted with Theophobia or treads a healthy path. Theophobia is not the same as a natural process wherein a person, seeking to find answers about the source of all life, questions whether God exits. Psychospiritual pathologies (*amrad ruhiya*) do not result from an honest search for answers about existence and consciousness. Far more destructive than physical anomalies, psychospiritual degeneration corrupts the soul, the *real* person. Normal physical decay is involuntary whereas psychospiritual pathology is *self-generated* and ultimately imperceptible to its victims.

> *They repel others from this (Quran), as they themselves stay away from it, and thus, they only destroy themselves without perceiving. (6: 26)*

> *Anyone who disregards the message of the Most Gracious, we appoint a devil to be his constant companion. (43:36)*

> *Do not be like those who forgot God, so He made them forget themselves. These are the wicked. (59:19)*

Theophobic Personality Disorder

The features of Theophobia and Theophobic Personality Disorder (TPD)[109] have been delineated in Divine revelation and echoed by those who are cognizant of psychospiritual pathology and abnormal personality. The features are:

1) Chronic attempts to suppress one's inborn awareness of God
2) Rejecting evidence of a Supreme Being or Intelligent Design in the makeup of the human and in creation
3) Chronic deliberate avoidance of spiritual themes (TPD)
4) Annoyance and hostility towards persons perceived as religious or spiritual
5) Promotion of philosophies and lifestyles that debunk or minimize spirituality
6) Engaging in rituals to "contact" Satan or other demonic forces (in the most severe types of Theophobia and TPD)
7) Ridiculing religious-minded individuals (TPD)
8) Exhibiting instrumental identification with a religion or spiritual system solely for social convenience or as a means to another end

In settings where religious or spiritual themes are not germane, Theophobia and TPD may not result in *overt* functional impairment. Theophobes may suffer from adjustment disturbances and features of mood, anxiety, and personality disorders.

In their minds there is a disease. Consequently, God augments their disease. They have incurred a painful retribution for their lying. (2:10)

Do you not see how we unleash the devils upon the disbelievers to stir them up? (19:83)

Unlike other psychological and psychiatric disorders, features of TPD are applauded in certain social settings and regarded as enlightened thinking and behavior. There are no medications or non-spiritual interventions for treating TPD. Individuals must muster the motivation and spiritual yearning to recover from Theophobia. This is possible only if a person sincerely chooses to relinquish disbelief in God. God is Oft-Forgiving and Most Merciful, but if an individual remains Theophobic to the moment of death, the soul exhausts its time in this life to submit to God, heal, and gain the spiritual strength to withstand the Presence of God.

God never burdens a soul beyond its means: to its credit is what it earns, and against it is what it commits. "Our Lord, do not condemn us if we forget or make mistakes. Our Lord, and protect us from blaspheming against You, like those before us have done. Our Lord, protect us from sinning until it becomes too late for us to repent. Pardon us and forgive us. You are our Lord and Master. Grant us victory over the disbelieving people." (2:286)

In the Quran, Theophobes are described as arrogant, misguided, straying in mind, mad, in the depths of darkness, hypocrites, false to themselves, delusional, ungrateful, diseased in their hearts, deaf, dumb, blind, and removed from spiritual Light. These traits are roughly analogous to exhibiting narcissistic features; being confused and disoriented about reality; being illogical and unreasonable; being mentally ill, ignorant, and deceptive; lacking insight and good judgment; and being spiritually estranged. Unlike many other mental illnesses, Theophobia cannot be divided into subcategories based on the number and type of features that a person exhibits. Any single specific feature of Theophobia, if maintained, is sufficient reason for the diagnosis. Theophobes are also deemed the "worst creatures" because they misuse their intelligence and ignore the inner Exalted Spirit.

Those who disbelieved among the people of the scripture, and the idol worshipers have incurred the fire of Gehenna forever. They are the worst creatures. (98:6)

Did they make an agreement with each other? Indeed, they are transgressors. (51: 53)

All creatures on the Chain of Being gravitate towards Unicity or the Great Absolute. Creatures in the animal kingdom do not deviate from their design and purpose, yet, spiritually wayward humans do. Theophobia is not identical to psychic illness primarily caused by neurogenic and developmental disorders nor to psychological maladies that result from problems in living, but Theophobic traits exacerbate such psychic illness. The relationship between Theophobia and emotional problems is an unknown to many students and practitioners of contemporary psychology, psychiatry, and counseling. Regarding themselves as normal and sane, Theophobes accuse those who are God-conscious of being old-fashioned, too religious, backward, and crazy.

The agreement between a Theophobe and his or her *internal* constant companion is an agreement to view anyone who values spiritual yearning as uninformed. A more common tactic is to promote the idea that healthy spirituality is not related to recovery from mental illness. This is analogous to a group of hospital patients who, after being apprised of the necessity for medical intervention, insist on leaving the hospital without treatment. Oddly enough, some hospital staff members believe that the patients should be discharged and compliment the patients on being assertive and taking matters into their own hands. One group is seen as healers, and the other group is seen as needing to be healed, but both the patients and staff exhibit shared psychospiritual maladies.

VIII

Adjustment And Personality

Prism of Beliefs, Feelings, and Thoughts

A prism slants or bends light that passes through it. A glass prism bends light beams into different spectrum colors. Lenses on cameras, camcorders, microscopes, eyeglasses, and telescopes are also prisms. Water is a simple prism. When a stick is placed in clear water, the portion of the stick beneath the surface appears to be bent. The illusion of a bent stick is caused by changes in the speed of light waves passing through air (one medium) then through the water (another medium). The image, not the stick, is distorted. Allegorically speaking, an individual's feelings, thoughts, and beliefs are housed in a prism of psychospiritual consciousness (the person's mind). Each person uses his or her prism of consciousness to 1) identify and label experiences and 2) navigate daily life. The clearer the prism, the more colors are displayed. In this analogy, in which the "prism" is the mind, colors signify important psychospiritual dimensions of an experience. The more prism colors there are, the clearer are an individual's perceptions in this time-space medium. The presence of only a few prism colors indicates distortions of reality. When a person seeks to become a Submitter Personality, God expands the person's consciousness so that the person can decipher the psychospiritual lessons of life experience. The nexus of consciousness, receptivity to Divine guidance, determines how well a person "reads" reality. In the Quran, phrases like "people who think," "people who reflect," "only the intelligent take heed," "people who understand," and "for those who possess intelligence" refer to people who have clear psychospiritual prisms. Individuals interpret and respond differently to the same situation because they look through different psychospiritual prisms.

Proclaim: "The bad and the good are not the same, even if the abundance of the bad may impress you. You shall reverence God, (even if you are in the minority) O you who possess intelligence, that you may succeed." (5:100)

Say, "Everyone works in accordance with his belief, and your Lord knows best which ones are guided in the right path." (17:84)

Say, "Whether you conceal your innermost thought, or declare it, God is fully aware thereof." He is fully aware of everything in the heavens and the earth. God is Omnipotent. (3:29)

In verse 17:84, the word *works* includes actions, reactions, deeds, responses, and performance. A person's thoughts, affect, attitudes, and actions are usually in accord with his or her beliefs. Aside from external supports, relief *is* in the belief and grief *is* in the belief. In others words, the cause of much grief and the solution to much grief rests in the extent that a person's beliefs and life perspective are in harmony with Divine guidance for humans. God alone knows a person's deepest thoughts and intentions. The primal *innermost thought* (3:29) underlies all conscious experience. A person's primal or original thought is either *"God is Omnipotent and my only Lord,"* or the person adopts a distortion of the innermost thought: *"I have doubts about God and His Power."* Regardless of whether a person voices his or her innermost thought or is aware of it, God knows it. Life is a series of tests designed to enable a person to act out his or her primal thought. After initially granting humans consciousness, God informed them that He alone is Lord and Creator. In turn, all humans bore witness that only God is Lord and Creator.

Recall that your Lord summoned all the descendants of Adam, and had them bear witness for themselves: "Am I not your Lord?" They all said, "Yes. We bear witness." Thus, you cannot say on the Day of Resurrection, "We were not aware of this." (7:172)

We created the human, and we know what he whispers to himself. We are closer to him than his jugular vein. (50:16)

After being placed in a human body, each soul acts out its thoughts, decisions, and beliefs. Based on his or her perceptions and interpretations, an individual decides whether to change his or her outlook and behavior. A person's outlook on life may or may not incorporate Divine guidance. In God's system, a person rejects Divine guidance when the person's prism of consciousness is tarnished, and as a result, the soul (the real self) shrinks. For example, because they committed themselves to disbelief in God's Power and Omnipotence, the people of Noah laughed at him as he constructed a small floating craft in a region devoid of heavy rainfall and without a large body of water. Lacking a reverence for God's Power and ignoring warnings, the people of Noah could not conceive of a flood where they lived. Given that his innermost and stated conviction was to worship God, Noah perceived his antagonists' behavior as absurd. Noah laughed at them for being so foolish as to dismiss God's Guidance and Power. Noah and his antagonists did not share the same beliefs, the same spiritual yearning, or the same fate.

While he was building the ark, whenever some of his people passed by him they laughed at him. He said, "You may be laughing at us, but we are laughing at you, just as you are laughing." (11:38)

Similarly, when the people of Noah disbelieved the messengers, we drowned them, and we set them up as a sign for the people. We have prepared for the transgressors a painful retribution. (25:37)

Moses' journey with his teacher illustrates the necessity for a person to heed counsel from those who are more knowledgeable and to beseech God to expand self-awareness (i.e., prism of consciousness). Blessed with knowledge and mercy from God, the teacher's psychospiritual prism was much clearer than Moses' consciousness. The teacher knew that few people understand situations beyond appearances. Devoid of sufficient knowledge about a situation, individuals draw hasty conclusions and opinions and behave in ways that may lead to harm rather than good. In each case along his journey with the teacher, Moses lacked the complete picture and was unwilling to listen to someone with more knowledge than him. Acceptance of God's plan in a situation only after all the information has been brought forward to satisfy the ego is not true submission. A successful person weathers life's ups and downs, trusts in God, exercises patience, maintains righteousness, and remembers to seek God's guidance in daily affairs.

The teacher told Moses that Moses could not endure what he could not understand. Because of his psychospiritual immaturity and impatience from the start of their journey, Moses was unable to grasp what the teacher was telling him.

Moses and the teacher eventually parted. God granted Moses guidance when Moses was *receptive* to the guidance and was no longer beguiled by his sense that he knew all the answers, had the best plan, and had the right perspective. God expanded Moses' consciousness so he could be guided and prepared to fulfill his prophetic mission.

> *They found one of our servants, whom we blessed with mercy, and bestowed upon him from our own knowledge. Moses said to him, "Can I follow you that you may teach me some of the knowledge and the guidance bestowed upon you?" He said, "You cannot stand to be with me. How can you stand that which you do not comprehend?" (18:65-68)*

> *The human being is impatient by nature. I will inevitably show you My signs; do not be in such a hurry. (21:37)*

Throughout life, individuals learn to adjust to different situations. Reasons why individuals cannot endure situations include age, limited mental faculties, lack of understanding, lack of experience, misguided single-mindedness, fear of truth, and a refusal to acknowledge that others know more about certain situations.

Personal Growth: A Divinely Guided Process

Each individual meets with good and bad situations that test the individual's spiritual mettle, emotional maturity, and faith in God. The concept of trial and test *(fit'nah)* includes desirable and undesirable circumstances, temptation, tumult, and situations warranting self-examination. *Fit'nah* varies in nature and degree according to God's plan for each person. Life tests are not restricted to one portion of humanity. No individual is without any limitations and faults, and no one is perfect or free of sin. *Fit'nah* affords each person opportunities to recognize and overcome blameworthy characteristics. The Creator assured each individual that He would not place any burden on the person that the person could not bear.

> *We will surely test you through some fear, hunger, and loss of money, lives, and crops. Give good news to the steadfast. When an affliction befalls them, they say, "We belong to God, and to Him we are returning." (2:155-156)*

God never burdens a soul beyond its means: to its credit is what it earns, and against it is what it commits. "Our Lord, do not condemn us if we forget or make mistakes. Our Lord, and protect us from blaspheming against You, like those before us have done. Our Lord, protect us from sinning until it becomes too late for us to repent. Pardon us and forgive us. You are our Lord and Master. Grant us victory over the disbelieving people." (2:286)

Every person will taste death, after we put you to the test through adversity and prosperity, then to us you ultimately return. (21:35)

We created the human being to work hard (to redeem himself). (90:4)

The assurance that The Creator does not overburden any soul is the bedrock of a balanced self-concept. A balanced self-concept enables an individual to meet life situations in a psychologically sober and stable manner rather than repeatedly claiming that he or she is helpless and unable to improve his or her life circumstances. A basic confidence that situations are *not* insurmountable is a source of inner strength and necessary for psychospiritual growth. Mature inner strength is cultivated and realized through submission to God.

The widespread use of the phrase *ego strength* in lieu of *inner strength* reflects the historical impact of classical psychoanalytic theory on Western psychology and popular culture. According to classical Psychoanalytic Theory, the ego keeps the id's uninhibited physical desires within bounds, and harnesses prohibitive inclinations of the superego. The id represents the impulsive part of the psyche that obeys the pleasure principle and seeks gratification of instinctual urges. The superego is a substitute for the spiritual conscience, and is supposed to represent the composite influence of ethical teachings, parental directives, and social expectations and standards. *Ego strength* refers to how well a person is able to maintain self-esteem with minimum conflict between the "harsh, demanding" superego and an "indulgent, pleasure seeking" id. The ego is like an arbiter or go-between that constantly must check the superego and the id. In spite of substituting the superego for the moral conscience, Freud later stated that "excessive judicial functions and demands" of the superego hinder rather than facilitate self-development.[110] No matter how hard he tried, Freud could not entirely escape the idea that moral guidelines for living are necessities of healthy life. At every opportunity, he shied away from the notion that the moral conscience is conducive to healthy personality development, though, in fact, a moral sense of right and wrong is essential to develop a healthy personality.

Failure to respond to situations in a balanced manner is due to 1) external constraints beyond the individual's control, 2) rejection or distortion of Divine guidance, 3) ignorance and immaturity, and 4) cognitive incapacity to cope with challenging situations. As long as a person staunchly rejects Divine guidance, healthy life adjustment is impossible. Each person made a covenant with God to seek solutions to life's difficulties and to use his or her intelligence in the right manner. Because of human weakness and limitations, mistakes and wrong decisions in life are unavoidable, but our Creator forgives struggling souls who sincerely yearn for the Truth. Even oppression is no excuse for the failure to seek Truth and strive toward self-realization (ta't'min un-nafs).

Yet, as regards those who fall in sin out of ignorance then repent thereafter and reform, your Lord, after this is done, is Forgiver, Most Merciful. (16:119)

I am surely Forgiving for those who repent, believe, lead a righteous life, and steadfastly remain guided. (20:82)

Those whose lives are terminated by the angels, while in a state of wronging their souls, the angels will ask them, "What was the matter with you?" They will say, "We were oppressed on earth." They will say, "Was God's earth not spacious enough for you to emigrate therein?" For these, the final abode is Hell, and a miserable destiny. (4:97)

Most willful non-productive attitudes and behaviors are mere rationalizations. In his book, *Why Am I Afraid to Tell You Who I Am?*, John Powell, S.J. posited a poignant and straightforward definition of rationalization.

Rationalization is the bridge that makes my wishes the facts. It is the use of intelligence to deny the truth; it makes us dishonest with ourselves. And, if we cannot be honest with ourselves, we certainly cannot be honest with anyone else. Rationalization consequently sabotages all human authenticity. It disintegrates and fragments the personality.[111]

With each new situation, an individual is challenged to use his or her intelligence to arrive at a healthy course of action. The brain and intellect cannot believe; they do not love or hate, nor are they biased. In a universe of beliefs, biases, and inclinations, the person (not the brain or intelligence) distorts or accepts truth. For some people, overcoming tendencies to distort truth is not an easy task. Self-honesty remains evasive for those who deny their spiritual yearning and rationalize away an innate desire to become a Submitter Personality. The compulsive rationalizer's life and actions are disconnected from an inner spiritual authenticity.

Do the people think that they will be left to say, "We believe," without being put to the test? We have tested those before them, for God must distinguish those who are truthful, and He must expose the liars. (29:2-3)

[W]homever God guides is the truly guided one, and whomever He sends astray, you will not find for him a guiding teacher. (18:17, partial)

Many forms of *behavior* maladjustment are reframed as psychological problems that beset individuals who are described as victims of factors beyond their control. For such persons, healthy adjustment to undesirable circumstances is presented as nearly impossible, without the intervention of trained professionals. Exaggerated interpretations of situations as unavoidable and insurmountable serve the ends of individuals attempting to circumvent personal accountability and professionals seeking to gain from individuals' alleged helplessness. Psychiatrist and author of *Reality Therapy*, Dr. William Glasser reached similar conclusions.

[Orthodox psychiatry] also avoids dealing with the issue of right and wrong. Deviant behavior is considered a product of mental illness, and the patient is often felt not morally responsible because he is considered helpless to do anything about it. The basic premise of Reality Therapy is almost the exact opposite. The patient's problem is seen as the result of his inability [or unwillingness] to comprehend and apply values and moral principles in his daily life.[112]

Individuals with emotional problems differ to the extent that they are willing to seek moral solutions to their difficulties and need professional and informal counsel from others. Regarding proper counsel, the Creator enjoins us to heed revealed guidance and ask those who know among us. The knowledgeable among us include individuals whose advice reflects knowledge of 1) Divine guidance, 2) fundamentals of mental health, and 3) healthy human adjustment. Acceptance of counsel from righteous parents, guiding teachers, and others who know is necessary to nurture the soul.

Small children and mentally handicapped individuals do not frequently experience adjustment disorders because they do not have the ability to grasp the dimensions of situations. However, prolonged stress can lead to childhood adjustment disorders. A child's understanding of reality is perfect for a child's developmental stage but necessarily inadequate for higher levels of information processing. *A person cannot respond to a situation until the person grasps the fact that he or she is in the situation. A person can only respond to aspects of a situation that he or she is aware of.* The more perceived aspects (i.e., colors in the prism analogy), the greater the personal awareness. Self-absorbed and eager to engage in laughter and play, children have an amazing ability to recoil from unpleasant circumstances. These qualities are a mercy and blessing from God. By contrast, many adults who have a greater grasp of situations do not choose to exhibit maturity and proper judgment. Neither children nor mentally handicapped, the people of Noah *chose* not to understand important aspects of the situation they were in.

It is the responsibility of those who know to do their part to safeguard the emotional well-being of vulnerable individuals. A friend's boyhood experience reflects how because a person cannot always grasp all aspects of a situation, it is important to be in the company of those who know. No more than five or six years old, the boy was with his parents on a train during a time when racial segregation was widespread in the United States. As the train stopped at a railroad station, the boy noticed that some passengers were preparing to get off the train. He wondered why he and his family did not get off the train as well and asked his mother why they remained on board. His mother smiled and replied, "We brought our own lunch." With that answer, the boy settled back and continued to enjoy the train ride. With age and maturity, he recalled the situation and could grasp details about it that he had been unable to recognize as a child. Certain themes emerged that had been beyond his awareness and grasp at the time the event occurred. He recalled that the individuals getting off the train were white, and in recalling the event as a grown man, he was now aware that as African-Americans, he and his family were not allowed to disembark from the train and eat lunch in the station. In his recollections of the situation, he read the signs posted in the railroad station—"Whites Only."

When the situation occurred, he could not read anything beyond a few words in children's storybooks. His mother's answer to his question was what he needed at the time. Had his mother said, "We are not allowed to get off the train because we are colored," her response might have planted the seed of doubt and an inferiority complex in his mind. Thus, by God's leave, his mother's response preserved the boy's healthy perception of his parents as in control of their own lives and his life.

> *We never burden any soul beyond its means, and we keep a record that utters the truth. No one will suffer injustice. (23:62)*

> *O you who believe, reverence God and utter only the correct utterances. (33:70)*

Adjustment Disorders

Precursors of Adjustment Disorders

When their natural and acquired wants are satisfied, individuals are pleased, but discontent comes when their wants are unmet. A person with an active spiritual yearning finds joy in situations that promote psychospiritual growth and is uncomfortable in psychospiritually toxic situations. In contrast, a psychospiritually estranged person experiences an illusory pretentious joy and solace in escape from God-consciousness but is annoyed when reminded of spiritual truth. Because they have committed themselves to God alone, God protects His servants from Satan's domination in their psyches.

> *"You have no power over My servants. You only have power over the strayers who follow you." (15:42)*

> *This is because they followed what angered God and hated the things that please Him. Consequently, He has nullified their works. (47:28)*

Individuals at greatest risk of suffering adjustment disorders are those who believe that satisfying contrived superfluous wants is essential to their well-being. *The ego interprets contrived wants as essential needs.* The preeminence of psychospiritually unhealthy desires reflects disorder.

Disorder means "disconnected from orderliness and stability." Psycho-emotional disorders are *disturbances* of and *disconnection* from a state of harmony and equilibrium (i.e., psychospiritual peace). Adjustment disorders are partly the result of being unprepared or unwilling to handle some unpleasant situations. A lack of preparedness may reflect an abrupt onset of unforeseen circumstances, faulty perceptions and misinterpretations of situations, and poor decision-making. Situations that are perceived as negative give rise to negative feelings. In some respects, the condition of a person who needs corrective visual lenses is similar to that of a person experiencing an adjustment disorder. Without wearing corrective lenses, a visually impaired person may frequently stumble, fall down, incorrectly estimate distances, have blurred vision, and be unable to read regular-sized text. In the case of an adjustment disorder, a person's feelings of stress, extreme emotions, distorted perceptions, and behavioral problems are equivalent to a visually impaired person's stumbling, falling down, and misreading information.

A person who needs corrective lenses has three options: 1) pretend that there is no problem with his or her vision, 2) acknowledge the need for corrective lenses but do nothing to acquire them, or 3) acknowledge the need for corrective lenses and take steps to get them. A person with adjustment problems also has three options: 1) pretend that there is no problem, 2) acknowledge displeasure with a situation but not change his or her outlook and behavior, or 3) acknowledge the problem and seek remedies to alleviate the problem.

Imagine the chaos that would ensue in a community if visually impaired individuals convinced themselves and others that none of them had vision problems. In a make-believe Sighted City, the "blind lead the blind" and regard stumbling, falling, reading problems, and blurred vision as normal. When violations of Divine guidance are deemed appropriate, psychospiritual stumbling, imbalance, and blindness become the norm, and adjustment disorders spiral. Additionally, these disorders are rarely addressed in the context of Divinely revealed remedies. Individuals who heed Divine guidance, though, learn from their mistakes, are receptive to correct advice, and overcome adjustment problems. No longer spiritually blind and visually impaired, they become seers.

Those who are righteous, whenever the devil approaches them with an idea, they remember, whereupon they become seers. (7:201)

The "approach" referred to in verse 7:201 occurs when a person becomes conscious of an idea or suggestion that violates God's guidance. Like a postal carrier bringing a letter to a person's house, Satan can *bring an idea or suggestion into a person's awareness.* When a nefarious idea enters the mind, the person's innermost thought *immediately* comes to mind. A healthy person remembers and accepts the correct innermost thought. A person who consistently wavers accepts a distorted innermost thought. With increasing rejection of the authentic innermost thought (i.e., *God is Omnipotent and my only Lord),* a person's adjustment problems increase in severity.

Mood Disorders

Most mood disorders are variants of depressive states. A person with a mood adjustment disorder is unable to maintain a sufficiently positive attitude and emotional state. The person does not modulate his or her thoughts and perceptions so as to recover from sadness, depression, and hopelessness. Mood disorders can be brief, waver incessantly between periods of mania and depression, or last for years. Grief and depression can be brought on by real or imagined stress, loss, abandonment, and victimization. Unresolved stress, grief, or bereavement may deteriorate into depression. The story of Jacob's reaction to the loss of his sons, Joseph and Benjamin, captures critical elements of depression and grief.

> He [Jacob] said, "Indeed, you have conspired to carry out a certain scheme. Quiet patience is my only recourse. May God bring them all back to me. He is the Omniscient, Most Wise." He turned away from them, saying, "I am grieving over Joseph." His eyes turned white from grieving so much; he was truly sad. They said, "By God, you will keep on grieving over Joseph until you become ill, or until you die." He said, "I simply complain to God about my dilemma and grief, for I know from God what you do not know. O my sons, go fetch Joseph and his brother, and never despair of God's grace. None despairs of God's grace except the disbelieving people." (12:83-87)

Although noted in revealed scriptures and ancient texts for thousands of years, science has now concluded that a person's moods and feelings significantly impact their physical well-being. More than fourteen hundred years ago, the specific relationship between depression, vision loss, and the immune system was described in the Quran (verses 12:83-87) in the context of Jacob's reaction to the absence of Joseph.

In the journal *Gerontologist*, Dr. L.G. Branch and his colleagues observed:

> *Vision loss is not only associated with functional problems but also with affective disorders* including lower morale, depression, social isolation, reduced feelings of self-esteem, diminished emotional security and low levels of social interaction.[113] (italics added)

In the *Journal of Behavioral Medicine*, Dr. Joseph Mercola noted that older men who are lonely often present with this psychosomatic syndrome as did Jacob who was clearly lonely in his grief over the absence of Joseph.

> For older men, feelings of depression may weaken the immune system…. In men, feelings of depression were linked to a diminished immune response. Most of the depressed feelings of men in the study arose not from actual clinical depression but from *feelings of loneliness*, the report indicates.[114] (italics added)

Dr. Mercola added:
> There are a number of different effective ways to address the stress. Certainly a strong spiritual foundation is one of the most important.[115]

In response to his sons' comments about his depression, Jacob told them that he had a strong spiritual foundation and placed his trust and hope in God. He said, "None despairs of God's grace except the disbelieving people." A Submitter Personality, Jacob understood that God would relieve him of his depression and grief. Jacob's patience and understanding constitute the most positive fail-safe belief or cognition to counter negative mood states.

> *If God supports you, none can defeat you. And if He abandons you, who else can support you? In God the believers shall trust. (3:160)*

A rapidly growing, emerging field called psychoneuroimmunology is leading to pivotal discoveries about the relationship between mood and physical illness. The new field includes elements of psychology, immunology, neurosciences, and related fields. Dr. David Beaton, a psychoneuroimmunologist, noted that mood impacts immune system functioning:

> Perceived mood also seems to play a role in immune system effectiveness. Having a positive attitude seems to correlate with an increased ability of the immune system in fighting diseases. In cases where patients have exhibited fear before a surgery, they have had a longer healing time afterwards. Correlations were observed in the number of lymphocyte cells and the person's level of optimism.[116]

Dr. Beaton cited another study that confirmed the effectiveness of a person's positive beliefs and mindset in overcoming the *rhinovirus*, the causative agent of the common cold.

> Even in relatively less dangerous health problems, mood can have an effect. A study with the common cold and emotions showed that participants with happy emotions exhibited a greater ability to fight off the cold when given a squirt of the rhinovirus.[117]

Anxiety Disorders

Anxiety is one type of *fear*. A person with an anxiety disorder lacks the ability to marshal sufficient internal resources to reduce real or imagined apprehension and anxiety. A natural emotion, fear serves a vital, life-preserving purpose. If humans had no ability to experience fear, humanity could not survive. Dangerous situations would not engender an avoidance or cautious response; individuals would blindly proceed into harmful situations that might cost them their lives. Despite it's usefulness in these situations, however, when it comes to distracting people from growing their souls, fear is Satan's most powerful tool.

> *It is the devil's system to instill fear into his subjects. Do not fear them and fear Me instead, if you are believers. (3:175)*

> *Is God not sufficient for His servant? They frighten you with the idols they set up beside Him. Whomever God sends astray, nothing can guide him. (39:36)*

Satan generates a special fear and anxiety among humans who choose his system. It is a *conditioned* fear of loss—loss of life, limb, possessions, position, group acceptance, personal advancement, favored relations, social contacts, and income. These concerns become idols when a person regards their safekeeping as more important than obedience to God. *In Satan's system, loss is associated with obedience to God, and gain with disobedience.* The horror of self-imposed unrepentant disobedience to the Supreme, Loving, Merciful Creator is obscured by satanic *implanted* fears. The most lethal fear is harboring a greater fear of anything other than the Creator. Submission and obedience to God nullify any fear or anxiety. The person knows that God alone *controls and knows* all things and provides for His creatures.

> *When the people say to them, "People have mobilized against you; you should fear them," this only strengthens their faith, and they say, "God suffices us; He is the best Protector." (3:173)*

> *Say, "I fear, if I disobeyed my Lord, the retribution of an awesome day." (6:15)*

Each loss that Satan uses to frighten and condition humans to ignore God's guidance is a distortion of the truth. Loss of life is a prevailing fear only as long as a person does not firmly believe that God creates all life and that this life is not True Reality, and as long as the person is unaware that termination of physical life does not constitute the death of the soul or real person since the human body is not the person. Furthermore, a human's physical life is terminated at the precise moment preordained by God. A person cannot delay or advance the moment of his or her physical death. Prophet Abraham's certainty in God's Power enabled him to enter the cremation flames that his father kindled to kill him. Many people lose limbs in all kinds of situations; many mystics subject their bodies to conditions that less developed souls regard as unthinkable. A person's physical body and limbs are not important for life in the eternal Hereafter. A fear of loosing favored status, social relations, position, and opportunities for advancement rests on the false belief that God is not Omnipotent, not All-Knowing, not the Source of all life, and not in total control of His creation, including each human being. The attempt to install this fear was illustrated in Pharaoh's threats to his magicians after they witnessed the miracles that Moses performed, by God's leave. Once connected to their true Lord, the magicians were oblivious to Pharaoh's threats to amputate their limbs, imprison them, and kill them. In the magicians' eyes, no threat or invitation of gain in this world could substitute for God's eternal Mercy and Blessing. The magicians realized that their existence was from God and *belonged to* God.

> *The magicians fell prostrate, saying, "We believe in the Lord of Aaron and Moses." He said, "Did you believe in him without my permission? He must be your chief; the one who taught you magic. I will surely sever your hands and feet on alternate sides. I will crucify you on the palm trunks. You will find out which of us can inflict the worst retribution, and who outlasts whom." They said, "We will not prefer you over the clear proofs that came to us, and over the One who created us. Therefore, issue whatever judgment you wish to issue. You can only rule in this lowly life. We have believed in our Lord, that He may forgive us our sins, and the magic that you forced us to perform. God is far better and Everlasting." (20:70-73)*

Animals and Humans: Similar Anxiety Responses

The behavior of livestock on their way to a slaughterhouse graphically conveys physical elements of anxiety. Sensing danger ahead, the fearful animals become uneasy and reluctant to move. Other animals exhibit similar behavior in the wild when they sense the presence of predators. When they see, hear, or smell a potential predator, herds blindly stampede at full speed away from the source of danger. In the Quran, the behavior of zebras is used as an analogy to describe Theophobes' behavior when they are reminded to accept spiritual truth.

> *Why are they so averse to this reminder? Running like zebras. Who are fleeing from the lion! (74:49-51)*

When fearful and worried, humans exhibit behaviors similar to those of frightened animals. The behaviors include startle responses, uneasiness, anxiousness, rigid compulsive behaviors, and hyper-vigilance. In animals and humans, fear reactions proceed from the autonomic nervous system that triggers the "fight or flight response," the impulse to wither defend oneself or escape. Unlike animals, in addition to reacting to real threats, humans exhibit various levels of anxiety and stress to imagined dangers.

God Relieves Submitters of Fear and Anxiety

The mother of Moses is another example of how God strengthens the hearts of those who experience anxiety and fear but seek relief in God.

We inspired Moses' mother: "Nurse him, and when you fear for his life, throw him into the river without fear or grief. We will return him to you, and will make him one of the messengers."…The mind of Moses' mother was growing so anxious that she almost gave away his identity. But we strengthened her heart, to make her a believer. (28:7, 10)

Not yet certain of God's power and control, Moses' mother was afraid and anxious when God commanded her to place her infant Moses in a basket in the Nile River. Because she was a Submitter, however, she obeyed God, although she remained fearful about Moses' welfare. In verse 28:10, God reveals that this situation had multiple purposes. One purpose was to allow Moses' mother to witness God's power and protection of Moses, and gradually elevate her to the status of spiritual certainty. Sincere individuals are escorted through life situations and their faith in God is transformed into certainty. Having attained certainty about God's Control, Omnipotence, and Omnipresence, such persons no longer experience fear and grief.

We said, "Go down therefrom, all of you. When guidance comes to you from Me, those who follow My guidance will have no fear, nor will they grieve. (2:38)

Say, "Nothing happens to us, except what God has decreed for us. He is our Lord and Master. In God the believers shall trust." (9:51)

Indeed, those who submit themselves absolutely to God alone, while leading a righteous life, will receive their recompense from their Lord; they have nothing to fear, nor will they grieve. (2:112)

According to Dr. Alfred Adler,[118] going from anxiety to contentment involves reducing the disparity between *what is* and what a person thinks *should be*. Dr. Adler proposed that a person experiences anxiety and frustration when what the person believes *should be is less than what is*. A person is temporarily satisfied when *what is exceeds what should be*. Yet, a person's limited expectations are not consistently realized in most situations. A person is content when *what is equals what should be.* Adler's observation mirrors the fact that when a person understands that God controls and knows all things, the person no longer experiences discontentment, anxiety, or mere satisfaction with fleeting states. God's Will reigns over submission to personal wants and wishes. With true contentment, there is no difference between God's Will and personal will. Contentment is a quality of Submitter Personalities.

Anything that happens on earth, or to you, has already been recorded, even before the creation. This is easy for God to do. Thus, you should not grieve over anything you miss, nor be proud of anything He has bestowed upon you. God does not love those who are boastful, proud. (57:22-23)

Relationship Disorders

A person with a relationship disorder has a problem establishing healthy bonds and interactions with persons with whom such bonds and interactions are expected. The genesis of many relationship disorders occurs in the first unit of orientation in this life—the family. The first relationships occur in the family, so other relationships are built on lessons learned and not learned in the family.

Across the ages, different cultures and societies have redefined the basic family unit to fit their needs. Nevertheless, in God's system, the family is first composed of a mother, a father, and children born of the marriage between the parents. Each member of a family is a unique individual. Parents share complementary (not competing) roles that enable the family to function in cohesion and harmony. Adopted children may become part of host families, and adopted children should retain their birth names, especially the names of their fathers. Whether born into families or adopted, individuals' souls are "assigned" to families. Individuals have a natural proclivity to want to know and establish contact with blood relatives. It is important to not make artificial distinctions between children in a household. Sibling rivalry and jealousy must be countered with consistent messages to treat each other with kindness. By God's leave, in the family setting, adults provide for and care for the helpless (their children). Parents provide for and protect their children, teach the young how to share, show love and concern for each other, teach their children proper boundaries and modesty, and encourage their children to develop their talents and worship God alone. Older siblings are entrusted with responsibilities in keeping with their abilities. Children model what they see, and guided parents set healthy examples for their children.

With the family as an anchor and refuge, parents escort their children into the outer world, imparting knowledge and understanding to their children in each situation they encounter. However, the perspective and knowledge of elders and forbearers should always be examined in the light of truth and new information. This is especially important regarding Divine guidance and the worship of the Creator. Unfortunately, in addition to their wisdom, parents also impart their ignorance to their children, attempting to persuade them to embrace false beliefs, negative behavior, and negative lifestyles. Conformity to false religious teachings is spiritually lethal. Each family member is an independent soul who will be held accountable for his or her actions on the Day of Resurrection. A person's respect for others in adulthood begins with learning to respect parents and older relatives and have respect for other family members. Children and adults are not equal in strength, life experience, understanding, knowledge, responsibilities, and wisdom. When biological or adoptive parents fail to carry out the most important functions and then treat their children either as equals or as subordinates in an abusive sense, problems are inevitable. In God's system, marked deviations from Divine laws of family life lead to negative inter-generational consequences. There are no quick fixes that can remedy the psycho-emotional damage and relationship problems brought on by early unwholesome intra-family relationships. In God's system, individuals who forgo superficial attempts at recovery and instead sincerely seek *psychospiritual recovery* are healed.

Quran Verses on Family and Extra-Familial Relationships

No family has ever met the picture of an "ideal family," While it is a shelter, a refuge, and a school of life, the family is not entirely removed from toxic influences and tests in this world. Yet, it is a mistake to attribute all of a person's adjustment problems in life to the person's family experiences. Like other revealed scriptures, the Quran has much to say about human relationships, starting in the family and branching out into the larger society. The following select verses from the Quran contain important and wholly accurate information about family life and wholesome relationships. The verses are quoted together with minimal commentary, so that each reader can glean information to further his or her understanding of Divinely revealed universal parameters of family life. Unlike man's endeavors to analyze and study the character of the human family, the guidance in the verses is not based on speculation and theoretical hypotheses about what constitutes healthy family life. Moreover, the knowledge is not limited to time, place, or culture.

Enjoin your children to worship the One God.
Moreover, Abraham exhorted his children to do the same, and so did Jacob: "O my children, God has pointed out the religion for you; do not die except as submitters." (2:132)

God created the procreation process; worship God and respect your parents.
O people, observe your Lord; the One who created you from one being, and created from it its mate, then spread from the two many men and women. You shall regard God, by whom you swear, and regard the parents. God is watching over you. (4:1)

Men and women have mutually complementary roles; a man should not beat his wife.
The men are made responsible for the women, and God has endowed them with certain qualities, and made them the bread earners. The righteous women will cheerfully accept this arrangement, since it is God's commandment, and honor their husbands during their absence. If you experience rebellion from the women, you shall first talk to them, then (you may use negative incentives like) deserting them in bed, then you may (as a last alternative) beat them. If they obey you, you are not permitted to transgress against them. God is Most High, Supreme. (4:34)

Do not murder your children; this includes abortion.
Losers indeed are those who killed their children foolishly, due to their lack of knowledge, and prohibited what God has provided for them, and followed innovations attributed to God. They have gone astray; they are not guided. (6:140)

God's Commandments
Say, "Come let me tell you what your Lord has really prohibited for you: You shall not set up idols besides Him. You shall honor your parents. You shall not kill your children from fear of poverty—we provide for you and for them. You shall not commit gross sins, obvious or hidden. You shall not kill—God has

made life sacred—except in the course of justice. These are His commandments to you, that you may understand." (6:151)

Do not worship or spoil your children.
But when He gives them a good baby, they turn His gift into an idol that rivals Him. God be exalted, far above any partnership. (7:190)

Children are a test.
You should know that your money and your children are a test, and that God possesses a great recompense. (8:28)

God created two sexes that join in marriage.
And God made for you spouses from among yourselves, and produced for you from your spouses children and grandchildren, and provided you with good provisions. Should they believe in falsehood, and turn unappreciative of God's blessings? (16:72)

Encourage family members to fulfill acts of worship.
He used to enjoin his family to observe the Contact Prayers (Salat) and the obligatory charity (Zakat); he was acceptable to his Lord. (19:55)

Enjoin family members to pray.
You shall enjoin your family to observe the contact prayers (Salat), and steadfastly persevere in doing so. We do not ask you for any provisions; we are the ones who provide for you. The ultimate triumph belongs to the righteous. (20:132)

Engage in chaste relationships.
Only with their spouses, or those who are rightfully theirs, do they have sexual relations; they are not to be blamed. (23:6)

Maintain the sanctity of the home.
O you who believe, do not enter homes other than yours without permission from their inhabitants, and without greeting them. This is better for you, that you may take heed. If you find no one in them, do not enter them until you obtain permission. If you are told, "Go back," you must go back. This is purer for you. God is fully aware of everything you do. You commit no error by entering

uninhabited homes wherein there is something that belongs to you. God knows everything you reveal, and everything you conceal. (24:27-29)

Maintain a proper dress code among family members and respect privacy.
O you who believe, permission must be requested by your servants and the children who have not attained puberty (before entering your rooms). This is to be done in three instances—before the Dawn Prayer, at noon when you change your clothes to rest, and after the Night Prayer. These are three private times for you. At other times, it is not wrong for you or them to mingle with one another. God thus clarifies the revelations for you. God is Omniscient, Most Wise. Once the children reach puberty, they must ask permission (before entering) like those who became adults before them have asked permission (before entering). God thus clarifies His revelations for you. God is Omniscient, Most Wise. (24:58-59)

Pray for the happiness of family members,
And they say, "Our Lord, let our spouses and children be a source of joy for us, and keep us in the forefront of the righteous." (25:74)

Luqman's lessons to his son is an example for parents.
"O my son, know that even something as tiny as a mustard seed, deep inside a rock, be it in the heavens or the earth, God will bring it. God is Sublime, Cognizant. O my son, you shall observe the Contact Prayers (Salat). You shall advocate righteousness and forbid evil, and remain steadfast in the face of adversity. These are the most honorable traits. You shall not treat the people with arrogance, nor shall you roam the earth proudly. God does not like the arrogant showoffs. Walk humbly and lower your voice—the ugliest voice is the donkey's voice." (31:16-19)

Men should not estrange their wives nor claim that their adopted children are their genetic offspring.
God did not give any man two hearts in his chest. Nor did He turn your wives whom you estrange (according to your custom) into your mothers. Nor did He turn your adopted children into genetic offspring. All these are mere utterances that you have invented. God speaks the truth, and He guides in the (right) path. (33:4)

Treat orphans with kindness and preserve their birth identities.

You shall give your adopted children names that preserve their relationship to their genetic parents. This is more equitable in the sight of God. If you do not know their parents, then, as your brethren in religion, you shall treat them as members of your family. You do not commit a sin if you make a mistake in this respect; you are responsible for your purposeful intentions. God is Forgiver, Most Merciful. (33:5)

Women can relax their dress code around close relatives.
The women may relax (their dress code) around their fathers, their sons, their brothers, the sons of their brothers, the sons of their sisters, the other women, and their (female) servants. They shall reverence God. God witnesses all things. (33:55)

Ask God to grant you righteous children; God assigns souls to families.
"My Lord, grant me righteous children." (37:100)

All humans were created from dust; and the human life span is predetermined.
He is the One who created you from dust, and subsequently from a tiny drop, then from a hanging embryo, then He brings you out as a child, then He lets you reach maturity, then you become old—some of you die earlier. You attain a predetermined age, that you may understand. (40:67)

The ultimate family is family of Submitter Personalities. Enjoin good relations.
The believers are members of one family; you shall keep the peace within your family and reverence God, that you may attain mercy. (49:10)

Family members do not always agree.
O you who believe, your spouses and your children can be your enemies; beware. If you pardon, forget, and forgive, then God is Forgiver, Most Merciful. (64:14)

Exhibit love and care towards your spouses.
Among His proofs is that He created for you spouses from among yourselves, in order to have tranquility and contentment with each other, and He placed in your hearts love and care towards your spouses. In this, there are sufficient proofs for people who think. (30:21)

Take care of your relatives.
This is the good news from God to His servants who believe and lead a righteous life. Say, "I do not ask you for any wage. I do ask each of you to take care of your own relatives." Anyone who does a righteous work, we multiply his reward for it. God is Forgiver, Appreciative. (42:23)

Righteous family members are reunited in The Hereafter.
For those who believed, and their children also followed them in belief, we will have their children join them. We never fail to reward them for any work. Every person is paid for what he did. (52:21)

Identity Disorders

A person plagued with an Identity Disorder has chronic difficulty acknowledging and accepting his or her self in the context of the secondary identities that the person assumes in life. For example, some individuals distance themselves from family members; others deny or have mixed feelings about their ethnic or cultural backgrounds; others question their value after retirement from their careers; and others are bewildered about the ultimate purpose of life and experience existential anxiety. Once a person understands that his or her original identity is that of a noble spiritual creature (i.e., soul), the significance of secondary identities pales. Despite their importance in this life, secondary roles and identities are not reflections of the true self (the soul). For example, a person may be a doctor, perform many civic duties and charitable acts, and have strong family ties but be at a loss when challenged to share his or her understanding of the real self. Adolescence is often viewed as the developmental stage rife with identity confusion. During adolescence, a person focuses on carving a personal identity apart from others, but the identity sought after in adolescence remains dependent on the group and social environment. It is a reactive identity. Each adolescent has a *unique reactive identity*.

A unique reactive identity is composed of roles and self-definitions that a person embraces in *response to external directives, expectations, and circumstances.* A reactive identity includes performing roles and adopting personas to merit approval, acceptance, and accolades from others. A reactive identity may also include habitually taking the opposite position of others (that is, consistently being "against" or "antisocial" or compulsively questioning what others accept). Depending on a person's beliefs and behavior, the person may convey the message, "I am what others are not," "I am what others and I expect me to be," or "I am unto my self" (distance from others). *A person's psychospiritual identity precedes and supersedes all reactive identities.* Amidst secondary identities, each individual should strive to "know thyself" in submission to God. In the context of performing his or her life roles, each person has opportunities to discover and nurture his or her psychospiritual identity. The transformation can be positive or negative. For example, in an individual's roles as a community member and mother or father, the individual may exhibit love and kindness towards children and respect for others. In the role of a teacher, a person should impart true information to students. To do otherwise harms the teacher's professional standing and harms the teacher's soul.

To overcome an Identity Disorder, a person should embrace attitudes, feelings, and thoughts conducive to *psychospiritual* contentment and peace. Attempts to "know thyself" when the self opposes Divine guidance shed light on a confused identity. Unfortunately, when the light shines on those inflicted with a confused, disordered self, some of them "turn the light off" and continue to ramble in existential bewilderment. Some claim that there is no such entity as a "self." According to them, the *self* that an individual experiences is a figment of the person's imagination, solely the product of neurological processes. Perplexed about how they became individual conscious beings, some individuals attempt to explain that "the self came from nothing." A psychospiritual Identity Disorder is the root cause of many *chronic* mood, anxiety, and interpersonal problems. Submitter Personalities do not suffer from identity problems. They also frequent the company of persons with active psychospiritual identities who grow their souls.

> *You shall force yourself to be with those who worship their Lord day and night, seeking Him alone. Do not turn your eyes away from them, seeking the vanities of this world. Nor shall you obey one whose heart we rendered oblivious to our message; one who pursues his own desires, and whose priorities are confused. (18:28)*

Medications Only Reduce Organic Symptoms

Psychiatric medication may reduce some neurobehavioral symptoms that accompany psychospiritual adjustment disorders, but true and complete relief from mood and anxiety disorders is ultimately realized in adopting positive beliefs and a lifestyle congruent with Divine guidance. God-given reason and common sense dictate that if psycho-emotional problems emerge from faulty beliefs, thinking, and feelings, a person who seeks healing should rid himself or herself of faulty beliefs, thinking, and feelings. The results of a recent study in the *American Journal of Psychiatry* on the impact of spirituality in the treatment of schizophrenic (i.e., psychotic) patients confirms that psycho-emotional illness and adjustment problems are best overcome when a patient's spirituality is incorporated in treatment. The authors concluded that a person's spirituality should no longer be considered a "strictly personal matter," not relevant to mental health treatment and recovery.

This study aimed to assess the role of religion as a mediating variable in the process of coping with psychotic illness.... For some patients, religion instilled hope, purpose, and meaning in their lives (71%).... Our results highlight the clinical significance of religion in the care of patients with schizophrenia. Religion is neither a strictly personal matter nor a strictly cultural one. Spirituality should be integrated into the psychosocial dimension of care.[119]

Complex Emotions Reflect Perceptions and Beliefs

He is the One who makes you laugh or cry. (53:43)

Created by God, human emotions emerge from the autonomic and central nervous systems. Emotions are unique elements of human consciousness and experience. Individuals smile and laugh when they have warm pleasant feelings, laugh at jokesters, laugh when they hear something humorous, laugh at what they regard as absurd, or even inappropriately mock others. Being imperfect, humans suffer psycho-emotional discomfort when frustrated, disappointed, faced with the consequences of their ill-thought-out and negative actions, and when they become victims. Individuals weep when in pain and in highly unpleasant situations, as a reaction to the loss of a loved one or treasured possession, and when facing the consequences of negative actions. People also weep when overwhelmed with strong positive emotions (e.g., rapture, joy, ecstasy). Feelings of profound love of God and joy in submission to Him bring some Submitters to tears.

Proclaim, "Believe in it, or do not believe in it." Those who possess knowledge from the previous scriptures, when it is recited to them, they fall down to their chins, prostrating. They say, "Glory be to our Lord. This fulfills our Lord's prophecy." They fall down on their chins, prostrating and weeping, for it augments their reverence. (11:107-109)

These are some of the prophets whom God blessed. They were chosen from among the descendants of Adam, and the descendants of those whom we carried with Noah, and the descendants of Abraham and Israel, and from among those whom we guided and selected. When the revelations of the Most Gracious are recited to them, they fall prostrate, weeping. (19:58)

When hungry, an infant cries. When fed and comforted, an infant becomes calm and quiet. As an infant matures, emotions become more complex. As the capacity for abstract reflective thought unfolds with age, emotions are associated with more complex experiences, ideals, principles, and beliefs. In their article, "The Animal That Weeps," neuroscientists Dr. Silvia Cardoso and Dr. Renato Sabbatini point out:

All animals with mobile eyes shed tears, *but only humans do so to express sadness, pain, or grief, in a process that appears to involve both our higher and lower brain centers.* Although the occasions and expressions of weeping vary across human cultures, crying is universal in human society…. Crying and laughing share central and peripheral expressive mechanisms in our brains and bodies. Both involve a *complex interaction among the prefrontal cortex,* limbic system, and the muscles and glands of the embryonic third branchial arch. Both also emerge as nonverbal communication by babies and later, in modified form, are incorporated into adult behavior. Neither appears abruptly in primate evolution; in nonhuman primates there are analogous behaviors, such as an ape's reaction to tickling and a rat pup's separation cry—although *humor and shedding tears to express complex emotion are unique to human beings.*[120]

Without emotions, uniquely human experience could not be possible. Emotions are part of being human.

Crying and laughing persist into later life because they are indispensable in expressing positive and negative feelings, inhibiting aggression, promoting social contact, and eliciting cooperative and helpful behavior. In this may lie the overarching explanation of both. What really matters about crying and laughing is understanding their roles in our lives. They are the unique human way of expressing strong emotions and convey a sense of commonality among all human beings.[121]

Individuals seek frames of orientation[122] and devotion to anchor their spiritual yearning, hopes, and aspirations. Depending on an individual's innermost thought and spiritual yearning, the individual finds solace and peace in pursuing the good or satisfaction in opposing Divine guidance. In her book, *Neurosis and Human Growth*,[123] Dr. Karen Horney conceptualized interactions between the self and the outer world as movement ignited by positive and negative feelings. Dr. Horney postulated that affect-driven movement is *towards, away, or against others*. A key element in the expression of such movement is what constitutes the "others." If the "other" is harmful, intentional movement *towards* indicates psychospiritual illness, ignorance, and an absence of correct guidance. Whereas, movement *away or against* reflects correct guidance and good judgment. If the "other" is beneficial, movement *towards* reflects guidance and good judgment. On the other hand, movement *away or against* indicates psychospiritual illness and ignorance. *Satan and jinn persuade (condition) willing individuals to anticipate gain and move towards what is spiritually harmful, and anticipate loss then move away and against what is spiritually beneficial.*

Fighting may be imposed on you, even though you dislike it. But you may dislike something which is good for you, and you may like something which is bad for you. God knows while you do not know. (2:216)

He promises them and entices them; what the devil promises is no more than an illusion. (4:120)

A disbeliever's psychospiritual movement towards the harmful and away [from] or against the beneficial is illustrated in an allegorical verse (24:39) in the Quran that describes a person in the middle of the desert thirsting for water. Truncated personalities move away from Divine guidance, and convince themselves that well-being lies exclusively in satisfying physical appetites and urges. The verse illustrates the process known as *apperception*—perceiving or interpreting something based on feelings, beliefs, and experiences. In the verse, a Theophobe thinks that his or her works will result in gain, only to be confronted with the reality that the works are in vain and God is ever-present.

As for those who disbelieve, their works are like a mirage in the desert. A thirsty person thinks that it is water. But when he reaches it, he finds that it is nothing, and he finds God there instead, to requite him fully for his works. God is the most efficient reckoner. (24:39)

Based on His knowledge of a person's innermost conviction, God controls a person's movement *towards* or *away and against* His guidance. As reflected in the Spiritually Inspired Self, God guides a person to love the Truth and move towards submission to Him.

And know that God's messenger has come in your midst. Had he listened to you in many things, you would have made things difficult for yourselves. But God made you love faith and adorned it in your hearts, and He made you abhor disbelief, wickedness, and disobedience. These are the guided ones. (49:7)

Absent spiritual guidance, unbridled human emotions are likened to a torrent of turbulent waves that eventually harken a vessel's ruin instead of balance in calm waters. Psychospiritually healthy individuals amend their unsteady emotions, beliefs, and behavior to overcome adjustment problems.

Surely, those who believe and lead a righteous life, the Most Gracious will shower them with love. (19:96)

They did believe, and we let them enjoy this life. (37:148)

With pain there is gain. Indeed, with pain there is gain. Whenever possible you shall strive. Seeking only your Lord. (94:5-8)

Life Is a Voyage

Amidst life's ups and downs, a healthy person learns to maintain an even keel. The nautical term *keel* refers to the underside of a boat or vessel that extends longitudinally along the center of a vessel's bottom. A keel is an apt analogy for the quality of a person's perceptions, reasoning, and spiritual yearning. Amidst waves and currents (i.e., life's ups and downs), a vessel's keel must float evenly on the water's surface to prevent the vessel from capsizing. Likewise, a person should try to maintain emotional and psychospiritual equilibrium amidst life changes. In the absence of equilibrium, the self capsizes or tips over in an unbalanced, disturbed (*maqlub*) state. Life is an interplay of situations that kindle a myriad of feelings (e.g., happiness, sadness, anger, disappointment, contentment, fear, courage, loneliness, etc.). Over time, these situations and feelings bring out a person's true spiritual conviction. Those who learn from experience, grow psychospiritually. Those who fail to learn have the option to reframe their perceptions and priorities or suffer the consequences of harboring unhealthy thoughts and feelings.

Anything good that happens to you is from God, and anything bad that happens to you is from you. (4:79, partial)

Do the people think that they will be left to say, "We believe," without being put to the test? We have tested those before them, for God must distinguish those who are truthful, and He must expose the liars. (29:2-3)

When we bestow mercy upon the people, they rejoice therein. But when adversity befalls them, as a consequence of their own works, they become despondent. (30:36)

The rudder of a vessel is used to turn it in a clockwise or counterclockwise direction on a surface. When a vessel capsizes, the rudder is useless. A rudder is an analogy for limited free will. The more disturbed and unbalanced the emotional and psychospiritual state, the less the person is able to make sound healthy judgments and decisions (i.e., turn the rudder in the correct direction). In the context of the keel and rudder analogies, life is a sea of feelings and thoughts, consciousness is the vessel, the keel is God-given reason and spiritual yearning, and the rudder represents daily choices and decisions. To reach the proper destination, a person needs to make the right decisions to stay afloat and on course. When the going gets tough, humans instinctively remember God, but frequently revert back to unhealthy behaviors and dismiss Divine guidelines for psychospiritual health.

When they ride on a ship, they implore God, devoting their prayers to Him. But as soon as He saves them to the shore, they revert to idolatry. (29:65)

When adversity afflicts the people, they turn to their Lord, totally devoting themselves to Him. But then, as soon as He showers them with mercy, some of them revert to idol worship. (30:33)

IX

The Self In Healing

Each person mirrors his or her spiritual state in daily experiences and has many opportunities to "grow" his or her soul. For example, every person who starts eating a meal does not instinctively express his or her spiritual yearning, but a person who is mindful of the One who provides all sustenance thanks God for nourishment of the body and the soul. *With each remembrance of God, a person's spiritual heart is healed and strengthened.* Each person's experiences are tailored so that the person can actualize his or her spiritual ambition—be it in light or in darkness. The Creator determined the nuts and bolts of actualization for each soul, and knows the earthly lifespan of each soul. Each person has sufficient time to allow his or her innermost spiritual convictions to find expression. In God's system, each individual's lifespan is preordained.

> *Thus, they said, "Is anything up to us?" Say, "Everything is up to God." They concealed inside themselves what they did not reveal to you. They said, "If it was up to us, none of us would have been killed in this battle." Say, "Had you stayed in your homes, those destined to be killed would have crawled into their death beds." God thus puts you to the test to bring out your true convictions, and to test what is in your hearts. God is fully aware of the innermost thoughts. (3:154)*

God knows each person's conscious, subconscious, unconscious, and preconscious thoughts. Imagine that you are producing and directing a movie. Prior to producing the movie, you know the actors, their thoughts and lines, the roles that they play in the movie, and their parting lines. What the actors are aware of and what they say in the movie reflect their conscious thoughts. You are also aware of the actors' subconscious thoughts that the actors have forgotten. The subconscious thoughts influence the actors and are just beneath the surface of their awareness. Unconscious thoughts have not yet entered the actors' awareness because they have not had the experiences that conjure them up. You are aware of their unconscious thoughts. Prior to joining the movie cast, each actor has pre-conscious thoughts about his or her role and commitment to the director. As the director, you know the actors' individual levels of commitment. Regardless of his or her station in this movie, each actor's performance is entirely in keeping with his or her promise to the director. In life, everyone entertains pre-conscious thoughts about submission to God prior to birth into this world. In the Hereafter, numerous souls will plead to return to this dimension to join the believers. Were they to return, such souls would again reject Divine guidance.

> *If only you could see them when they face the hellfire! They would say then, "Woe to us. Oh, we wish we could go back, and never reject our Lord's revelations, and join the believers." As a matter of fact, (they only say this because) their secrets have been exposed. If they go back, they will commit exactly the same crimes. They are liars. (6:27-28)*

Prior to this life, individuals chose to remain psychospiritually ill or undergo psychospiritual recovery. The healable decided to repent and heed Divine guidance. It is God's Mercy to remove our memory of our individual decisions to worship or not worship Him alone. *The healable are healed.* In the absence of healing (through genuine repentance and reverence of God), the self becomes Theophobic, complex-ridden, and ego-driven. When asked the question, "Do you want to heal?" a hospitalized person in denial replies, "You certainly are not talking to me. There's nothing wrong with me!"

Hardened Spiritual Hearts

A hardened physical heart is not an operational distribution system for the oxygen-filled blood that a living organism needs. Imagine that hardened blood vessels are like damaged electric cords. Without contact with an electrical current, an electrical device cannot function. The device may be brand spanking new but, short of repairing the electric cord, the device is not viable. The spiritual heart hardens when a person relinquishes the capacity to receive and retain spiritual light, the lifeblood of the soul.

Leave from the Divine Presence

This hospital *(mashfan)* called earthly life is a "mash unit" *for psychospiritual healing and treatment (shifaa ruhiya and istish'faa ruhiya).* The Creator designed and constructed the hospital to provide humans with countless signs, opportunities, and experiences to recover from doubt about God's existence, authority, and omnipotence. In the context of life circumstances, human and jinn patients are given their last chance to re-educate themselves, denounce their egos, repent, and be redeemed by submitting to God's absolute authority. The Supreme Healer *(Al-Shafee)* composed full-proof prescriptions and guidelines for patients. *An inspired patient engages in productive self-examination and learns how to meet life circumstances in a healthy manner.* Echoing the Quran, Shuwardi cautioned:

> Man should, therefore, spend the few days he has on earth to transform the precious jewel of his soul into the image of an angel and not into that of an animal.[124]

Figure 6.1 (page 88) illustrates how a person *loses psychospiritual balance.* Figure 8.1 (page 121) depicts a person's psychospiritual *condition.* The Submitter Personality is depicted in the upright top position (i.e., psychospiritual health). The healable are guided back to the upright position (i.e., souls in the image of angels). Departures from the upright position lead to the states and conditions noted in the left and right quadrants. Variations of those states and conditions range from mistakes to severe psychospiritual states. The more a person departs from the upright position, the more frequent are the person's troubles and adjustment problems. Although offered treatment in the hospital *(mashfan),* patients with hardened spiritual hearts regress below a recuperative threshold where they are psychospiritually decapitated. Invisible to the physical eye, the decapitation is recognized in the form of psychospiritually lethal conditions; characteristics of those lethal conditions are noted in the bottom quadrant.

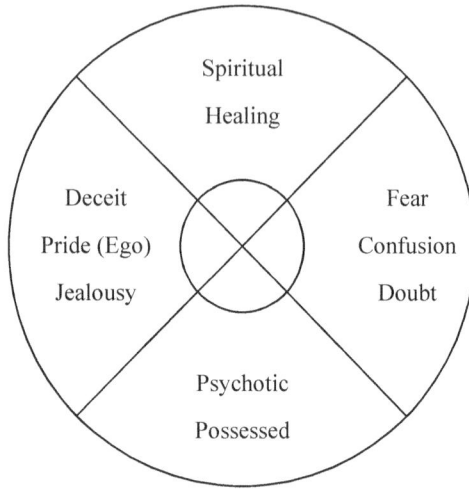

Figure 9.1. Axis of Psychospiritual Illness and Healing

Dr. Muhammad Abdul-Hadi Abu Reidah's article, "Physical and Psychological Health in Islam," explains how man's dual spiritual/physical nature while in this hospital either contributes to his healing or, if marred, contributes to his suffering. Drawing from the writings of the tenth century Islamic scholar, Abu 'Ali Ahmad Ibn Maskaweyeh, Dr. Abu Reidu wrote:

> Man has two sides: a physical side that makes him fit with the world of animals and a spiritual side that makes him fit with angels. Sensory pleasure is uninteresting and temporary although man has a natural disposition for it because of its commanding power. If the sensory pleasure masters man, it will control him, and make him approve of every evil. On the other hand, mental pleasure is permanent, though man has no natural disposition for it at first. However, if man trains himself he will discover its beauty and magnificence and will eventually come to love it…. [M]an [is either] in a state of physical pleasure and happiness but eager for spiritual pleasure [Spiritual Yearning] and furthermore seeking it, or he is in a state of spiritual pleasure and happiness, regarding physical pleasures as a manifestation of Divine wisdom. In the first state, man cannot live a life free of troubles whereas in the second state he is just like the angels.[125]

The chronic troubles that Dr. Abu Reidu described are rooted in cleavage from the Exalted Spirit. Through healing (i.e., receptivity to Divine guidance), a person's bond with God's Truth strengthens, and psychospiritual complexes gradually give way to inner peace.

Anyone who works righteousness, male or female, while believing, we will surely grant them a happy life in this world, and we will surely pay them their full recompense (on the Day of Judgment) for their righteous works. (16:97)

Those who submit completely to God, while leading a righteous life, have gotten hold of the strongest bond. For God is in full control of all things. (31:22)

Spiritual Healing Removes Psychospiritual Complexes

In *Individual Psychology*,[126] Dr. Alfred Adler noted that humans are born with distinctly human *superiority and inferiority feelings*. The superiority feeling gives rise to a child's belief that "I can do and become whatever I want to do, and I am somebody!" A complement of the superiority feeling, the inferiority feeling is a sense of incompleteness, of not yet being full, complete, or whole. A child with an inferiority feeling about riding a bike might utter, "I've got to learn how to ride my bike. I don't have enough experience riding it yet." Parents and adults attempt to cultivate children's superiority and inferiority feelings in a manner consistent with the parents' and adults' view of wholesomeness and personal strength. When it comes to psychospiritual growth, the adages, "the eldest is the wisest" and "experience is the best teacher," do not apply. Regardless of elders' beliefs and practices, each patient is enjoined to take his or her own psychospiritual medication. Many patients in this hospital choose not to heed psychospiritual guidance. Prophet Abraham's experience with his father and community is an example that each person is responsible to seek Divine guidance, irrespective of prevailing Theophobic practices in a community.

Each person experiences anxiety-producing life situations that may give rise to *superiority and inferiority complexes*. Negative complexes emerge as a function of accommodating a self conditioned to *fear* rejection and disapproval from groups and individuals. By forsaking spiritual truth, people grant their egos license to impersonate them, but when individuals embrace Divine guidance, they can discern the difference between their lordly (pure form) souls that seek healing and their complex-ridden ego impersonators. Most psychospiritual complexes emerge as a function of ignorance, arrogance, and immaturity.

Have you seen the one whose God is his own ego? Will you be his advocate? (25:43)

Spiritual awareness is excruciating to spiritually anesthetized patients. They avoid mention of the Supreme Healer (*Al-Shafee*) and prefer superficial respite from their psycho-emotional problems. Despite differences in age, language, geographical origin, customs, cultures, and life circumstances, "stubborn" patients suffer from *identical* psychospiritual maladies born of egotism and listening to their jinn companions.[127] *The self in healing (nafs shufiya) learns to recognize the difference between true sustained calm and peace, and fleeting, superficial euphoric states that only mask toxic thoughts and feelings.* Analogous to rocks from whence none or various amounts of water may gush forth, some spiritual hearts are completely closed to spiritual light, some hearts permit the full entrance of spiritual light, and some hearts only open to receive a degree of spiritual light.[128] *The healing elixir is spiritual light from God, The Supreme Healer-Physician. The healing process is psychospiritual personality development.* In the light of Divine guidance, personal demons and psychological complexes are extricated.

O people, enlightenment has come to you herein from your Lord, and healing (shifaa'un) for anything that troubles your hearts, and guidance, and mercy for the believers. (10:57)

We send down in the Quran healing (shifaa'un) and mercy for the believers. At the same time, it only increases the wickedness of the transgressors. (17:82)

Acknowledging the Need for Healing and Guidance

Complex-ridden spiritually anesthetized patients regard God-consciousness as equivalent to an obsessive neurosis. Behaving as if subjected to a tyrant's dictates, spiritually anesthetized patients distance themselves from Divine guidance. In contrast, souls in healing are blessed with conscientious contact with the Exalted Spirit. *The self in healing recognizes that without God's guidance and reassurance, a person becomes psychospiritually ill.* For example, Abraham asked God to reassure his heart and remove his doubt about life after death. Abraham's words as to who healed him when he was physically ill also apply to psychospiritual weakness.

"And when I get sick, He heals me (fa'huwa ya<u>sh</u>'feen)." (26:80)

Abraham understood that the first step in healing is to acknowledge *the need to be healed, the need for help.* The next step is to seek help from The Almighty One who can heal you. Like their counterparts who utter similar words, Submitters who follow the Quran recite "The Opener" (*Al-Fatihah*) daily and repeatedly ask God for help.

You alone we worship. You alone we ask for help. (1:5)

Without Divine help and healing, order, design, and harmony would be nonexistent. Everything receives counsel or guidance commensurate with its purpose, nature, and potentials. When Pharaoh asked Prophet Moses who was his lord:

He said, "Our Lord is the One who granted everything its existence, and its guidance (hadayaa)." (20:50)

A variation of *hidayat,* the word *hadayaa,* means "to give counsel, to show the way, to give direction along a path, to guide." If heeded, the guidance awakens reflective God-consciousness. In humans, *hadayaa* includes giving direction to an individual's lordly soul. The person heeds Divine laws for living, his or her conscience Law-Abiding Self, a central sense, reasonable advice, and counsel from others. God is the Supreme Guide. In the Inspired Self, characteristics of the lordly soul are brought forward. Residing in this life's biochemical hospital gown, an individual who refuses to be healed becomes impervious to psychospiritual guidance.

The self in healing knows that God guides His servants who choose to be guided. Through submission to God alone, one attains the authentic superiority feeling— love of God and anticipation of eternal happiness. *The thirst for happiness is a quality of the soul.* Sincere patients do not tire of asking for Divine guidance to overcome impulses to stray off the path of healing. In God's recovery system, an individual's personality mirrors his or her healing. Distant from the recovery system, a self dominated by toxic impulses gradually folds and fractures under the weight of the ego and lack of spiritual Light.

When My servants ask you about Me, I am always near. I answer their prayers when they pray to Me. The people shall respond to Me and believe in Me, in order to be guided. (2:186)

He is the One who places contentment into the hearts of believers to augment more faith, in addition to their faith. To God belongs all forces of the heavens and the earth. God is Omniscient, Most Wise. (48:4)

Prayer and Healing

Salat, an Arabic word that means "prayer," also means "contact." Merely assuming physical postures and making vocalizations do not constitute spiritual contact with the Existence of God. Millions of people in the three monotheist faiths (Judaism, Christianity, and Islam) and other religions perform variations of the *contact prayers* originally revealed to Prophet Abraham. The *intention* of prayer originates in the mind (spirit), whereas physical movements join the spiritual and physical worlds. Divinely ordained physical positions and movements should not be ignored or altered. *Notwithstanding the necessity of obligatory physical moments, spiritual contact occurs in the spiritual dimension.* Contact prayer protects, heals, humbles, reminds, and enables a supplicant to glorify God *in the manner that God prescribed.* Prayer on "my own terms" when and how "I want to do it" is a weak signal at best. It does not constitute submission to God because it is not on God's terms according to His Divine system. The Creator knows more about human nature and each human soul than humans can ever know about themselves.

In the absence of *sincere* prayer and contemplation of God, nothing immediately happens, at least outwardly; however, an individual becomes increasingly susceptible to prompts to widen the disconnect from submission to God. Prayer and other reverential duties become more difficult to perform. Non-performance of religious duties no longer engenders uneasiness. A person's mind is bombarded with justifications that encourage the person to ignore his or her spiritual yearning and religious duties. When a person who sincerely yearns to submit to God is attacked with evil thoughts, the person seeks refuge in God.

Failure to pray and connect with the Exalted Spirit leads to preoccupation with this life and seeking actualization solely in this world. Human souls that fail to nourish their spiritual connection during this life are unable to return to God's Presence. A caterpillar (insect larva) is a potential moth or butterfly. Imagine a caterpillar that steadily eats, but does not eat ingredients critical to its future transformation. The caterpillar initially experiences innate signals to correct its diet but ignores the signals. The inner signals eventually dim, and the caterpillar continues to eat the wrong sustenance. In the human realm, "wrong sustenance" can be regarded as faults that beset the individual who ignores the inner Exalted Spirit. At the specific period in its life when it should spin its cocoon, the caterpillar is unable to spin one. If the caterpillar manages to spin a cocoon, it is unable to later emerge from the cocoon as a healthy moth or butterfly. During its crawling larva stage, the disconnected caterpillar ignored signals to align its movements and diet with its higher nature. Unable to attain full development, the caterpillar is confronted with non-retractable *arrested transformation*. The natural process that enables the caterpillar to become a butterfly is halted by the caterpillar's decisions and actions. In this analogy, the caterpillar represents a person and his or her actions, the foliage denotes Divine guidance for self-development or misguidance that detracts a person from true self-development, the cocoon reflects transition from a wayward self to self-knowledge, and the moth or butterfly signifies a healthy developed soul or personality. Fortunately, caterpillars and other creatures cannot oppose their inborn natures. In misusing the languages of the scientific method and mental processes, misguided mental health professionals have significantly contributed to arrested human psychospiritual transformation.

A disconnected caterpillar is like a person who believes that the characteristics of a healthy personality are popularity, charisma, physical appearance, and satisfaction attained exclusively through indulging his or her desires. This person never attends to his or her inner exalted signal that transcends the physical self that is undergoing cellular decay and renewal. With the exception of cells in the cerebral cortex, all other cells in an adult body may be no more than seven to ten years old. It is crucial for a person to nourish his or her soul (i.e., psychospiritual self) through prayer, other Divinely ordained acts or worship and positive thoughts and actions. Otherwise, the person ends up like the metaphorical disconnected caterpillar. An individual with a fractured soul will be free of the cocoon or crypt of this life but unable to re-enter the Presence of God (i.e., Heaven). No longer imprisoned in what the twelfth century Muslim philosopher and mystic, Sheik Mubyi al-Din Suhrawardi, called the "crypt of the cosmos,"[129] the person's real self is subjected to eternal anguish. This is a reminder of an ageless Divine instruction to humans to "remember our true home." Individuals forget, then remember, and then hopefully decide to eat the right psychospiritual "foliage"—the remembrance and worship of the Creator.

O you who believe, you shall reverence God and seek the ways and means to Him, and strive in His cause, that you may succeed. (5:35)

As physical strength and the transitory radiance of physical life recede, a disconnected self becomes preoccupied with attempting to maintain a fantasy and facade of physical youthfulness and psychological well-being. Unable to maintain the fantasy and façade, the disconnected self plunges into despair and hopelessness. After observing hundreds of people from different cultures and walks of life, the late psychiatrist Erik Erikson characterized the last stage of human life as a sense of either integrity or despair. With advanced age, individuals become more dependent, grow weak, suffer memory loss and, possibly, forms of dementia, and seem to return to states of relative helplessness. Persons with a sense of having lived a righteous life experience Integrity in their later years. With death's approach, each soul rises joyfully or has to be "forcibly snatched" out of this "crypt of the cosmos."

God is the One who created you weak, then granted you after the weakness strength, then substituted after the strength weakness and gray hair. He creates whatever He wills. He is the Omniscient, the Omnipotent. (30:54)

Whomever we permit to live for a long time, we revert him to weakness. Do they not understand? (36:68)

The (angels who) snatch (the souls of the disbelievers) forcibly. And those who gently take (the souls of the believers) joyfully. And those floating everywhere. Eagerly racing with one another—to carry out various commands. (79:1-5)

Contemplative Healing

Positive thoughts, reflection, observation, study, and meditation are facets of contemplative healing. Each human "larva" must heed inner signals to recuperate from psychospiritual illness. As depicted in Table 8.2, a young person (i.e., infant or child) in Stage I perceives without experiencing higher emotions or sentiments. In the first two years of the hospital stay, the infant mind stores sense perceptions and simple associations that increase in complexity on a daily basis. The Exalted Spirit abides in infants, children, and mentally handicapped individuals, and it may come as a surprise that some of their thoughts about God far exceed, in genuineness and purity, their older brethren's thoughts about the Creator. A person grasps only what he or she is capable of grasping.

Table 9.2 Stages of Contemplative Psychospiritual Healing

Stages	Qualities
I: Pre-Recognition	An infant or small child perceives without recognizing order, beauty, and design. In this stage, a person has not developed the cognitive capacity to recognize and appreciate features of the outer world or ponder the origin of and interworkings of things.
II: Recognition/ Non-Recognition	Person recognizes order, beauty, and design in creation. This inborn distinctly human capacity and curiosity remains active throughout life. Individuals who choose not to heed their spiritual yearning do not advance beyond this stage. Despite their knowledge, they suppress their innate awareness of the existence of the Creator.
III: Awareness of Creator	Person is escorted across the threshold from awareness of lawfulness and order in creation to awareness of a Creator. While many individuals attain Stage III, their awareness of a Creator is muddled with false spiritual traditions and practices.
IV: Self-Realization	Person seeks *full* psychospiritual recovery, healing, and redemption; worships the One God, attains self-realization and peace, and strives to become a Submitter Personality.

In Stage II, a person experiences wonderment and appreciation of the beauty, design, and order in creation. Appreciation and inspirational feelings beckon a willing person to continue to seek out more design, beauty, and order. Ceasing to seek psychospiritual healing, some people do not cross the threshold into Stage III. In the context of life as a hospital for human souls, such persons do not move from critical urgent care to the recovery room. Their observations, study, and contemplation are confined to the hospital's nooks and crannies.

In the creation of the heavens and the earth, and the alternation of night and day, there are signs for those who possess intelligence. (3:190)

In Stage III, a seeker is *escorted* across the threshold from the created to the Creator. The escorts are angels who inspire human souls to seek God and find peace in submission to God. Recall the analogy of a person in a room illuminated by a lamp. Along with surveying what the light makes visible, many people seek to discover the source of light, beauty, and order in their rooms. They realize that the source is not the lamp or what the lighted lamp makes visible in their rooms, but the light itself. Heeding their Spiritual Yearning, they realize that there is a Divine Being. Stage IV is attainment of transcendence and self-knowledge. Stage IV individuals long to experience the deep love for, reverent thoughts about, and sublime feelings that accompany a realized connection to the One God.

Those who proclaim: "Our Lord is God," then lead a righteous life, the angels descend upon them: "You shall have no fear, nor shall you grieve. Rejoice in the good news that Paradise has been reserved for you." (41:30)

From the psychospiritual perspective, personality development begins the moment a person asks him or her self the perennial question: "What or who am I?" Each person also asks: "Where do I fit in the scheme of things?" and "Where am I ultimately headed?" In pursuit of answers to these questions, each individual's personality starts to take shape. Only a conscious spiritual being contemplates, ask questions, and seeks answers. The Creator gave human souls garments (human bodies) to wear in this world, special equipment (higher consciousness, common sense, intelligence, conscience, and limited free will), and commanded humans to "Read" throughout the journey. In this context, "Read" means to read and heed God's revealed messages, and acknowledge His signs in one's self and throughout creation.

Read, in the name of your Lord, who created. He created man from an embryo. Read, and your Lord, Most Exalted. (96:1-3)

As previously discussed, some individuals insist that there is no Creator and no higher purpose underlying human existence. Regarding the theory that life emanated from accidental forces, scientists who are true to the scientific method and unbiased in their quest for answers about the origin of life have proved that the theory is false. Confirmed by an in-text miraculous mathematical Code, the Quran repeatedly states that creation, including human life, are the products of a Divine Designer. The Creator revealed complete essential information about healthy personality development, and causes of psychospiritual illnesses. Endowed with the Exalted Spirit, individuals journey through life stages laden with challenges, opportunities, and situations that ignite their innate awareness of God. Commensurate with each person's level of understanding, the stages herald in a myriad of thoughts, emotions, and beliefs about experiences and the meaning of life. Unlike distances traveled on a physical path, a sojourner's inner growth is reflected in the enfoldment of his or her *psychospiritual* personality. Passage in this life is akin to being in a hospital where patients can individually choose to recover from psychospiritual illness and estrangement from the Creator. A higher inner signal constantly beacons humans to seek healing and learn the right answers to the three questions.

Each Patient: A Psychospiritual Seeker

Irrespective of background, if a person genuinely seeks to know and act on the right answers, he or she will, by God's will, heed the signal and mature into a Submitter Personality. In his or her innermost being and preconscious, each patient wants to return to the Divine Presence. In their innermost being, individuals who are intoxicated with the crypt of the cosmos and seem impervious to the idea of life after death actually know that the human journey extends beyond this world. Personality is *not matter*. The false self's fleeting preoccupations with indulging the ego disguised as the true self *do not matter*. In the tradition of sincere spiritual teachers, yearners, and seekers, Sheik Abdullah Ansari (1005-1090 C.E.) recognized that when a soul genuinely seeks the Truth, *it comes to know itself, and loves the One who created it.*

It is held that when a Seeker gives his heart and mind to the search, and disperses the mists that arise from tumultuous passions, Truth becomes brighter and fills the soul with its light. It is asserted that while reason is puzzling itself with the mystery of consciousness, time and space, the man of Truth is going forward from discovery to discovery, in the growing illumination of his heart.... The seekers of Truth, therefore, concentrate all their strength in drawing away the mind from sense objects and to set it free from the dominations of fear and hate. Some follow the path of knowledge and others the path of devotion, hoping to lose all sense of duality in the supreme uprising of love.[130]

The Creator teaches each soul that consciously submits to His Will that it is no less than the luminance of the sun and the lunar light of the moon, the alternation of day and night, the grandeur of the celestial heavens, and this earth's beauty. Humanity has been shown the two paths. Ultimate success lies in recovery and redemption from evil. *Psychospiritual actualization is the grand recovery and redemption that takes place when a person accepts the right answers to the three questions.* The soul's final abode is in a boundless spiritual habitat of eternal joy or misery. As spiritual larvae in this life, individuals choose to emerge as Submitter Personalities or truncated souls unable to return to God's Presence. By God's grace, those who are healed and redeemed participate in the supreme uprising of Eternal Love.

Subsequently, his Lord chose him [Adam], redeemed him, and guided him. (20:122) Successful indeed is the one who redeems his soul. By remembering the name of his Lord and observing the contact prayers (Salat). (87:14-15)

By the sun and its brightness.
The moon that follows it.
The day that reveals.
The night that covers.
The sky and Him who built it.
The earth and Him who sustains it.
The soul and Him who created it.
Then showed it what is evil and what is good.
Successful is one who redeems it.
Failing is one who neglects it. (91: 1-10)

Glossary

Afaa To wipe out or remove in order to restore to health

al-fit'ra Innate inborn nature of a species or life form

Al-Musawwir The Supreme Designer, an attribute of God

An-Naf'saaniya Science of the self, psychology

Al-mus'taqeem Path (sirat) of piety and righteousness

Aql Apprehension, the capacity to perceive the meaning of what enters a person's awareness

Ash-Shakh'saniya Science of personality, personality theory

ash-shawq ur-ruhi Spiritual yearning, longing, or desire to connect with the Source (God, Exalted Spirit) of life, impulse towards contact with God

dalal Psychospiritual estrangement, to go astray, mental confusion

dhikr To remember, recollect, commemorate; the invocation of God

far'daa Individual, single, or separate; each person's unique personality

fit'nah Life tests, circumstances when an individual chooses to cultivate spiritual yearning or oppose God's guidance

hadayaa To give counsel, to show the way, to give direction along a path, to guide

himmat Aspiring, inspired, to have high aims and goals.

hiss mush'tarik Central or common sense that enables a person to experience reality

hubb 'ad dhat Self-love, self-centeredness, narcissism

ih'san Human being, mankind

ilm un- nafs Self-knowledge, self-awareness

Islam (aslama) Peace, submission (to God), religion of creation

jihad un-nafs Self-struggle, inner struggle to overcome negative behavior and the false self

Jinn. Spiritual creatures that were created from an invisible fire or energy unknown to man. Wayward jinn are descendents of Satan (i.e., devil). Each time a human is born, a jinn (*genii* in English) is assigned to that human as a lifelong companion who attempts to convince (but not force) the human that Satan's point of view (i.e., God is *not* Absolute, All-Knowing and All-Powerful) is correct

Junun Spiritual psychosis, a psychotic mental condition

Kibr Conceit, vanity, haughtiness; an attribute that is not perceived by others unless a person expresses it in behavior

maj'nun Possessed, psychotic, mentally ill, psychospiritual disease

maj'zub Mental illness in the innermost realm (i.e., soul) of the psyche or consciousness, when a person succumbs to inner enticements and suggestions to violate Divine guidance

maq'lub Inverted from upright position; disturbed, an unbalanced state of mind

marid Sick, ill, diseased

marid nafsi Psychopath, sociopath

ma'rifat un-nafs Highest plane of self-knowledge or consciousness; gnosis, union with Absolute Consciousness

mashfan Hospital, used in the context of the earthly life as a hospital for the soul

mukaabara Stubborn, obstinate

mujaddid Renewer or reformer

mushahada To witness, to see, to testify, self-examination

nafs Self, soul

nafs ad-dalla Self that wonders, oscillates back and forth, and alternates between inner states and circumstances, as in a circular motion without guidance

nafs al-kalimah Self that is perfected as a Mercy from God, a reward for souls in God's Presence, soul that is made pure, unsullied, and brought near to God

nafs al-lawwamah Self that abides by laws and follows rules, self-regulation; heeding the conscience, self that heeds God' commands and acts within parameters of laws and guidelines

nafs al-qana'ah Self that is satisfied, content, moderate and temperate in affairs, also at peace with God's provisions, free of tensions and fear of loss, does not exhibit envy and jealousy, the soul is fully content in seeking God's provision prescribed for it

nafs al-radiyah Self that is satisfied, happy and pleased, soul is pleasing to God

nafs kafarah Self that hides, covers, and attempts to supplant the truth, an unbelieving self or atheist; self that seeks and chooses the wrong path in life, God seals the person's mind and heart from recognizing spiritual truth

nafs mujaddah Restored and rejuvenated self in submission to God, a person who attains self-knowledge

nafs mul'hima Self that is inspired and motivated to please God, the self sees God's approval and being in His Presence as the highest state, righteous actions are not "driven" by fear of punishment or mere worldly reward

nafs mut'mainna Calm peaceful Self that hopes to be admitted into God's Presence after this life, and its deepest satisfaction is the love of God

nafs shifaai Self in healing from psychospiritual illness, yearns to have a Submitter Personality

nafs ath-thala Self that is lost and astray from God's guidance, this self goes beyond mere vacillation between states and chooses misguidance and deception (i.e., *tath'leel*) as a way of life

qalb Heart or mind, innermost consciousness

Quran Revealed to Prophet Muhammad in 570 A.D., the verses of the Quran were released from Muhammad's heart over the course of twenty-three years. The Quran consists of 114 chapters, with chapter lengths ranging from three verses to two hundred and eighty-six verses. In 1974, a 19-based miraculous mathematical Code was discovered embedded in the original Arabic text (final written sequence) of the Quran. Not one letter can be added to or deleted from the text of the Quran without it being immediately exposed. Even with the aid of the most advanced computers, the Code cannot be imitated or reproduced

Ruh Spirit

Ar-Ruhihi Spirit of God

Ruhu 'l Insan Human spirit

Ruhu 'l Azam The Exalted Spirit (i.e., Spirit of God) that God breathed into man, God alone knows the nature of the Ruhu 'l Azam

Salat Prayer that establishes connection or contact with God

Shifaa Cure, healing, restoration, recovery

shakh'siah Distinctive personality, character, or identity

shirk Idolatry, polytheism, to add something (to someone or something)

shirk-ul-'Adah Polytheism of undutifulness to God by engaging in concocted rituals, beliefs, rites, and superstitions

shirk-ul-Ibadah Polytheism of undutifulness regarding the worship of One God

shirk-ul-'Ilm Polytheism of undutifulness to the Source of all knowledge, the act of literally ascribing the ultimate source of knowledge to anything other than God

shirk-ut-Tasarruf Polytheism of undutifulness to the Source of all power, control, and influence, belief that anyone or anything shares power with God or the notion that God is lacking in power, control, and influence

tabaq Stage, phase, developmental stage

taj'deed Reformation, renewal, restoration of something or someone

takabbar Arrogance, excessive pride (i.e., external expression of conceit), superiority complex

that'leel Deception, misguidance, factors that promote deviation from Divine guidance

taz'kiyah Development of good self that was created in the best design, disciplining of evil self

was'wasi Whisper, prompt, or subtle suggestion, Satanic suggestion or temptation

rashad Reason, good sense, maturity

quwwat al-khayal Faculty of imagination

zallaam Person who embraces evil or opposes upright nature and Divine guidance

Index

P

Paradise
26,28,65,84100,103,150
Parents
3,24,25,30,34,51,59,81,86,100,103,116,117,126,127,
128,130,143
Patients
95,102,109,121,133,141,143,144,145,151
Path of righteousness (*as-sirat al-mus'taqeem*)
58
Personality theories development (*taz' kiyah*)
35
Pharaoh
123,145
Pieper, Josef
37
Pius XII, Pope
39
Plaisted, David
8
Plants (*nabata*)
72
Powell, John
115
Praise to God
69,93,95,96,99
Prayer (*salat*)
59,129,130,152
Preconscious
Psychoanalytic theory
Psychology
130,140,151
Psychopath (*nafs marid*)
102
Psychopathology (*maj'nun*)
55
Psychosis (*junun*)
101
Psychospiritual pathologies (*am'rad ruhiya*)
106

References and Notes

1. M. Bucaille, *The Bible, the Quran, and science*. Translated by D. Pannell Alastair (Elmhurst, New York. Tahrike Tarsile Press, 1995). Also see: C. Taslaman, *The Quran: Unchangeable miracle*. Translated by Ender Gurol (Eden, South Dakota: Nettleberry Publications, 2006).

2. Rashad Khalifa, *Quran: The final testament* (Revised Edition II) (Fremont, CA: Universal Unity Press, 2000). Verses of the Quran cited in *Self-Knowledge and Spiritual Yearning* are from Dr. Khalifa's translation. In 1974, Dr. Khalifa (1936-1990) discovered a miraculous mathematical Code embedded in the original Arabic text of the Quran.

3. F. Abate, *The Oxford American desk dictionary* (New York: Oxford University Press, 1998). This dictionary is used as the English language reference in this book.

4. Erich Fromm, *Man for himself* (New York: Henry Holt & Co., 1947), Chapter 4.

5. Syed H. Nasr, *An introduction to Islamic cosmological doctrines* (Albany, NY: State University of New York Press, 1994), 72-73.

6. The great physicist Dr. Albert Einstein said, "Science without religion is lame, and religion without science is blind." From: "Albert Einstein Quotes," http://quotations.home.worldnet.att.net/alberteinstein.html

7. Wikipedia information about Dr. Edwin Conklin from the Wikipedia online article "Edwin Conklin." In 1936, Dr. Conklin was president of the American Association for the Advancement of Science.

8. "Gems of Thought," (on-line article), http://www.soultrek.com/quotes.html

9. Advocates for teaching "ape-to-man evolution" argue that students have a right to be exposed to a so-called scientific theory of the origin of man. It is unethical and academically incorrect to present theories replete with speculation and fudging of evidence as models of scientific inquiry in classrooms.

10. C.S. Hall & G. Lindzey, *Theories of personality* (New York: Wiley and Sons), 1957.

11. Ted Byfield, "Another jolt for evolution theory," *Science Prabhupada Hare Khrisna News Network,* 2000, http://science.krishna.org/Articles/2000/10/00169.html.

12. J. G. West Jr., "Darwin in the classroom," *National Review Online*, December 2002, http://www.discovery.org/scripts/viewDB.

13. W.C. Schefler, *Biology: Principles and issues* (Reading, MA. Addison-Wesley Publishing Co., 1976), 15.

14. Quran verses 29:19-20 and similar verses were an inspiration behind the creation of sciences such as paleontology, geology, and anthropology.

15. Michael Denton, *Evolution: A theory in crisis* (Adler and Adler Publishers, 1996), 264, 338.

[16] Ibid.

[17] The "cell city" analogy can be found in biochemistry textbooks and on the Internet. Visit the website entitled, "Cellcity." http://www.biopic.co.uk/cellcity/index.htm.

[18] John Reader, "Whatever happened to Zinjanthropus?," *New Scientist*, 15, (1981), 802-805.

[19] W. Smith, *Teilardism and the new religion* (Tan Books and Publishers, Inc., 1988), 8.

[20] L. Stubbs, "How closely related are mice and men?," *Human Genome Project Information* website - Functional and Comparative Genomics Fact Sheet. http://www.ornl.gov/sci/techresources/Human_Genome/faq/compgen.shtml.

[21] D.A. Plaisted, "The human genome revealed," http://www.cs.unc.edu/~plaisted/ce/genome.html.

[22] AllaboutGod Ministries, "DNA double helix – information code," http://www.allaboutscience.org.

[23] B.Carey, "Cosmic 'DNA': double helix spotted in space by space telescope," http://www.space.com/scienceastronomy/060315_dna_nebula.html.

[24] Michael J. Behe, "Evidence for intelligent design from biochemistry," Paper presented at the meeting of the Discovery Institute's God and Culture Conference, 1996. http://wiki.cotch.net/index.php/Michael_Behe.

[25] M. J. Behe, *Darwin's black box.* (New York: Touchstone Press, 1996), 39.

[26] Creation Science Facts, "DNA and cells," http://www.pathlights.com/ce_encyclopedia/08dna03.htm.

[27] Alice Bailey, *The Consciousness of the atom* (New York: Lugis Publishing Company, 1961), 38-39.

[28] Albert Einstein, *Cosmic religion* (New York: Covici-Freide Publishers, 1931), 98.

[29] Ibid., 22.

[30] C.B. Worthman and E.F Loftus, *Psychology* (*New* York: Alfred A. Knopf, Inc., 1981), 285.

[31] Ibid. 284-285.

[32] For a condensed description of the Ikwan al-Safa, see the article: Nader El-Bizri, "Brethren of purity," The Institute of Ishmaili Studies, http://www.iis.ac.uk/home.asp?l=en.

[33] S. H. Nasr, *An introduction to Islamic cosmological doctrines* (Albany, NY: State University of New York Press, 1994), 61.

[34] Ibid. 69.

[35] Claire Bradon, "Not so Dumbo - elephant intelligence," Science and Nature, http://bbc.co.uk/nature/animals/features/302feature1. (From an original article in the August 2003 issue of *BBC Wildlife* Magazine). Research studies and articles about the intelligence of elephants are available on the Internet.

[36] S. H. Nasr, *An introduction to Islamic cosmological doctrines* (Albany, NY: State University of New York Press, 1994), 61.

[37] Ibid.72

[38] Ibid.73, 74.

[39] T.P. Hughes, *Dictionary of Islam* (Lahore, Pakistan: Shah Nawaz Press, 1885), 547.

[40] Quran verse 22:5 is a detailed description of human pre-natal development. The Arabic word "ih'san" means "human." The word's geametrical value is sixty-five (65). The words dust, drop, hanging, lump of flesh, bones, and flesh are in verse 22:5. The words occur 17, 12, 6, 3, 15, and 12 times in the Quran. The sum of these numbers is 65, the geametrical value of the word "ih'san."

[41] C. Taslaman, *The Quran: unchallengeable miracle*. Translated by Ender Gurol (Eden, SD: Nettleberry, LLC, 2006), 147-148.

[42] Ibid.

[43] Y. Petty, "Chromosomes and genes," http://www.ncc.gmu.edu/dna/dna.htmDNA.

[44] The atomic number is the number of protons in the nucleus of an atom.

[45] A miraculous mathematical code is embedded in the original Arabic text of the Quran. For information about the code, go to: http://masjidtucson.org and http://www.submission.org.

[46] J.N. Bleibtreu, *Parable of the beast* (New York: Macmillan Press, 1968).

[47] Muller, A., *You shall be a blessing* (San Francisco: The Alfred Adler Institute, 1992), 5.

[48] Ibid, 4.

[49] W. Meader, "Upliftment: self quotations-the self and God," http://www.meader.org/articles/Upliftment.htm.

[50] Wilhelm Wundt, *Principles of Physiological Psychology* (First Edition, 1874). Excerpt from web article, "Reading, 'Riting and Rats," http://www.freedommag.org/english/vol36i1/page08.htm#3b.

[51] E. Fromm, *The sane society* (New York: Henry Holt and Co., 1955), Chapter 9.

[52] A. Muller, *You shall be a blessing* (San Francisco: The Alfred Adler Institute, 1992), 3.

[53] P. Yogananda, *The science of religion*. (Los Angeles: Self-Realization Fellowship, 2001), 69-70.

[54] Ikhwan Al-Safa, The cosmos and the hierarchy of the universe, 74.

[55] Joseph Pieper, *The four cardinal virtues* (Notre Dame, IN: University of Notre Dame Press, 1966), 50.

[56] J.M. Cowan, *A dictionary of modern written Arabic* (London: MacDonald & Evans Ltd., 1974). This dictionary is used as the Arabic language reference for this book.

[57] Carl J. Jung, *Psychology and religions* (New Haven, CT: Yale University Press, 1963), 61.

58   The word *teleological* (from Greek *telos*, "end"; *logos*, "reason") refers to purpose, end, and final causality. In the context of human life, it means to be designed to fulfill a purpose devised by a Mind that transcends nature.

59   T. Rosario, *The philosophy of life: The pope and the right to life* (Warren, NH: Pro Fratribes Press, 1989), 57.

60   James E. Royce, The internal senses. In *Man and his nature: A philosophical psychology* New York: McGraw-Hill, Inc., 1961), 72.

61   Gordon Allport, *Becoming a person* (New Haven, CT: Yale University Press, 1961), 229.

62   S.J. Idris, *The Process of Islamization* (Maryland: International Graphics Printing Company, 1977), 4.

63   Evil mentation constitutes intentional thoughts and prompts to engage in criminal immoral activities including harm to others and to self, violations of Divine guidance, and bizarre or "crazy" behavior.

64   S.H. Nasr, *Science and civilization in Islam* (New York: Plum Books,1968), 223.

65   The notion of human "races" is unscientific and an invalid descriptor of human differences. In relation to the technical classification of life forms, the word *race* means "species." Human beings constitute a single species. The use of the term *race* to describe different groups of people is a social construct that has lead to considerable confusion and misunderstanding between ethnic groups.

66   In 1980, the American Psychiatric Association listed "Multiple Personality Disorder" as a formal diagnosis in the Statistical Manual of Mental Disorders (DSM-III). Some therapists and researchers purported to have identified such a disorder. In 1994, the disputed diagnosis was renamed "Dissociative Identity Disorder" (DID). The description of DID remains the same as in "Multiple Personality Disorder"— "the presence of two or more distinct identities or personality states that recurrently take control of behavior…. [with] a distinct personal history, self-image, and identity, including a separate name (p. 484)." As clarified in the Quran, an individual does not have two or more distinct identities or personalities states.

67   "The HU in secular texts," The HU page, http://www.sourcetext.com/hupage/

68   Author unknown, *The laws of Manu*, Translated by Wendy Doniger and Brian K. Smith (London: Penguin Books, Ltd., 1991), 153.

69   T.P. Hughes, *Dictionary of Islam* (Lahore, Pakistan: Shah Nawaz Press, 1885), 547.

70   S.M. Qutb, "The Islamic basis of development," *Islam and development* (Plainfield, IN: Association of Muslim Social Scientists, 1977).

71   Carl Rogers, *On becoming a person* (New York: Houghton Mifflin Company, 1961).

72   G.J. Manaster, and R. J. Corsini, *Individual psychology.* (Chicago: Adler School of Professional Psychology, 1982).

[73] Victor E. Frankl, *Man's search for meaning* (New York: Simon and Schuster: Washington Square Press, 1963).

[74] E Erikson, *Childhood and society* (New York: Norton Press, 1963).

[75] A.H. Maslow, *The further reaches of human nature* (New York: Viking Press, 1972).

[76] E. Fromm, *Escape from freedom* (New York: Henry Holt and Co., 1994).

[77] The highest motivation behind self-development should be to please the Creator of the self rather than simply becoming what one thinks is good and desirable to one's self. Despite appearing confident and assured, the self that has no hope of God's acceptance cannot be pleased with itself.

[78] D. Rosser-Owen, "Social change in Islam: the progressive dimension," *The Muslim Institute Papers* (SloughBerk, UK: Open Press, Ltd., 1978), 19.

[79] M Valliuddin, *The essential features of Islam* (Hyderabad, India: Da'iratu'l Ma'arif Press, no publication date given), 89.

[80] Dr. Jung recognized that many psychiatric problems are a result of not cultivating spiritual yearning, and rejecting the psychospiritual solace provided by a personal connection to the Creator.

[81] Abu Hamid al-Ghazzali (1111 A.D.) was one of the greatest scholars in the history of Islam. Al-Ghazzali's scholarship and writings had an indelible influence on Medieval European scholars. The Catholic scholastic order known as the Jesuits read and preserved al-Ghazzali's works in the original Arabic. Al-Ghazzali's *Ihya Ulum ad-Din* (Revival of the Religious Sciences) is regarded as a masterpiece on the self (*nafs*) and psychospiritual development. His *Mishkat al-Anwar* is a commentary on the Verse of Light (24: 35) and the Verse of Darkness (24: 40) in the Quran.

[82] C.B. Wortmann and E.F. Loftus, *Psychology* (New York: Alfred A. Knopf, Inc., 1981), 248-249.

[83] Derived from the Arabic root *labisa*, the name "Iblis," denotes one who obscures, confuses, and enjoins doubt by means of deception and disguise. Iblis behaved exactly in this manner to deceive Adam and Eve.

[84] F. Abate, (Ed.), *The Oxford American dictionary*. (New York: Oxford University Press, 1998).

[85] These dimensions of creation that God controls are derived from verses of the Quran.

[86] A.H. Al-Ghazzali, *Mishkat al-Anwar*. Translated by W.H.T. Gardner (Lahore, Pakistan: Sh. Muhammad Ashraf Press, 1952).

[87] S.A. Latif, *The mind Al-Quran builds* (Hyderabad, India: The Willa Academy, 1971).

[88] Malik Badri, *Contemplation: An Islamic psychospiritual study* (Cambridge: Cambridge University Press, 2000), 28, 79.

[89] R.M. Bucke, *Cosmic consciousness* (New York: E.P. Dalton Press, 1923).

90 Molecular biochemists have discovered that the plant genome is very similar to the human genome. See Garritano, T. (2001). *Plant genome offers clues to longevity: Arabidopsis can survive the loss of an enzyme that prevents aging.* National Science Foundation Online. http://www.findarticles.com/p/articles/mi_pfsf/is_200103/ai_2098986286.

91 No person alive in the sixth century A.D. could have known that plants and humans have similar genome structures, nor would anyone have detailed knowledge of human prenatal development.

92 Alice Bailey, *The consciousness of the atom* (New York: Lucis Publishing Company, 1974), 87-89.

93 Frank Abate, *Roget's II The new thesaurus* (New York: Houghton Mifflin Company, Third Edition, 2003), 383.

94 Karen Horney, *The neurotic personality of our time* (New York: Norton and Company, Inc., 1964).

95 This fear is frequently misinterpreted as a pervasive "existential anxiety"—a sense of nothingness, emptiness, and despair that besets individuals who ignore their spiritual yearning.

96 Ibid.

97 A.H. Abdel-Kader, *The life, personality, and writing of Al-Junayd* (London: Luzac and Company, Ltd., 1976), 175.

98 The related word, "*Naf'saaniya,*" means "psychology" or the science of the self.

99 P. Yogananda, *The science of religion* (Los Angeles: Self-Realization Fellowship, 2001), 21.

100 C.G. Jung, *Modern man in search of a soul* (New York: Harcourt, 1933), 264.

101 *A History of Muslim Philosophy.* (Chapter 19). http://www.muslim philosophy.com/chp19.doc.

102 Recall that the "human spirit" (*Ar-Ruhu'l Insani*), is sometimes united to the body, and sometimes separated from it, as in sleep or death; it is the conscious and intelligence. The *"Exalted Spirit"* (*Ar-Ruhu 'l-Azam*) is connected to the existence of God.

103 Angels wholly submit to God. When offered free will, they chose to relinquish it, fearing the consequences of having an ability that, once misused, would distance them from God. Angels' first and only act of free choice was to reaffirm their unswerving submission to the Creator. Contrary to myth and folklore, angels are not humans with wings nor or they human-like in appearance. While not corporeal beings, angels can assume human form upon entry into this world. Under the absolute control and command of God, angels are the dispatchers of Divine revelation. In total accord with God's system, they protect humans, record the deeds of each individual, drive the winds, regulate natural forces, and effectuate and oversee all motion and phenomena in this dimension.

104 R. Khalifa, *Quran: The final testament* (Fremont, CA: Universal Unity Press, 2000), Introduction, XV.

REFERENCES AND NOTES

[105] J.E. Rychlak, *Personality and psychotherapy: A theory-construction approach* (Boston, Mass: Houghton Mifflin Company, 1981), 188.

[106] R. D. Hare, *Without conscience* (New York: The Guildford Press, 1993), 81.

[107] C. G. Finney, "Moral insanity," *Oberlin Evangelist* (Lecture VII), 1856.

[108] Webster's Revised Unabridged Dictionary (1913), http://www.konline.com/moral_insanity.html.

[109] All features need not be present in an individual who suffers from Theophobia. Features identified with the designation (TPD) are characteristics of TPD.

[110] W.S. Sahakian, (Ed.), *Psychology and personality* (Chicago: Rand-McNally Publishing Co., 1997), 7-11.

[111] J. Powell, *Why am I afraid to tell you who I am?* (Allen, TX: Thomas More Publishing, 1998), 98.

[112] W. Glasser and L.M. Zunin, "Reality therapy," In R. Corsini, *Current psychotherapies* (Itasca, Illinois: F.E. Peacock Publishers, Inc., 1973), 304-305.

[113] L. Branch, A. Horowitz, and C. Carr, "The implications for everyday life of incidents of self-reported visual decline among people over age 65 living in the community," *Gerontologist, 29,* 1989, 359-365. http://www.amdalliance.org/information/depression/literaturereview.php.

[114] J. Mercola, "Depression and anger affect the immune system," *Journal of Behavioral Medicine*, 24, 2001, 537-555. http://www.sites.mercola.com/2002/jan/19/depression/_anger.htm.

[115] Ibid.

[116] D. B. Beaton, "Effects of stress and psychological disorders on the immune system," http://www.personalityresearch.org/papers/beaton.html.

[117] Ibid.

[118] G. Manaster and R. Corsini, *Individual psychology: Theory and practice* (Chicago: Adler School of Professional Psychology, 1982).

[119] S. Mohr, P. Brandt, L. Borras, C. Gilliéron, and P. Huguelet, "Toward an integration of spirituality and religiousness into the psychosocial dimension of schizophrenia," *American Journal of Psychiatry,* 163, 2006, 1952-1959.

[120] S. H. Cardoso, and R. M.E Sabbatini, "The animal that weeps," In S. H. Cardoso, (Ed.), *Brain and mind*, 16, December 2002- April 2003. http://www.cerebromente.org.br/indexge_i.htm.

[121] Ibid.

[122] E. Fromm, *The sane society* (Greenwich, CT: Fawcett Premier Book, 1968).

[123] K. Horney, *Neurosis and human growth: The struggle toward self-realization* (New York: Norton and Company, Inc., 1950).

[124] (Author unknown), "A History of Muslim Philosophy," http://www.muslimphilosophy.com/hmp/chp19..doc., 393.

[125] M. Abu Reida, "Physical and psychological health in Islam," http://www.islamset.com/hip/Abu Reida.

[126] Adler, A. (1968). *The practice and theory of individual psychology.* Totowa, NJ: Littlefield, Adams, and Co.

[127] Ansbacher, H.L. and Ansbacher, R.R. (Eds.) (1956) *Individual psychology of Alfred Adler: a systematic presentation in selections from his writings.* New York: Basic Books.

[128] Despite the fact that many psychological illnesses are the result of problems in living, some mental health professionals aggressively promulgate biochemical interventions as primary remedies for anxiety, depression, self-doubt, and identity confusion.

[129] Suhrawardi's "crypt of the cosmos" is a beautiful description of the state of the soul separated from its home, and temporarily "entombed" in this life. http://www.muslimphilosophy.com/chp19.doc.

[130] R. Khalifa, "Aphorisms of Sheik Abdullah Ansari," *Islam: An international journal expressing the Islamic point of view,* 1 (1), 1974, Back inside cover.

Bibliography

Abate, F., *The Oxford American desk dictionary* (New York: Oxford University Press, 1998).

Abdel-Kader, A.H., *The life, personality, and writing of Al-Junayd* (London: Luzac and Company, Ltd., 1976).

Abu Reida, M., "Physical and psychological health in Islam," http://www.islamset.com/hip/Abu Reida.

Adler, Alfred, *The practice and theory of individual psychology* (Totowa, NJ: Littlefield, Adams, and Co., 1968).

Al-Ghazzali, Abu Hamid, *Mishkat al-Anwar.* Translated by W.H.T. Gardner (Lahore, Pakistan: Sh. Muhammad Ashraf Press, 1952).

Allport, Gordon, *Becoming a person* (New Haven, CT: Yale University Press, 1961).

Ansbacher, H.L. and Ansbacher, R.R. (Eds.), *Individual psychology of Alfred Adler: a systematic presentation in selections from his writings* (New York: Basic Books, 1956).

"A History of Muslim Philosophy," (Chapter 19), http://www.muslim_philosophy.com/chp19.doc.

Badri, Malik, *Contemplation: An Islamic psychospiritual study* (Cambridge: Cambridge University Press, 2000).

Bailey, Alice, *The consciousness of the atom* (New York: Lugis Publishing Company, 1961).

Beck, Aaron T., *Cognitive therapy and the emotional disorders* (New York: Penguin Books, Inc., 1979).

Beck, A. T. & Emery, Gary, *Anxiety disorders and phobias: A cognitive perspective* (New York: Basic Books, 1985).

Behe, Michael J., *Darwin's black box* (New York: Touchstone Press, 1996).

Bleibtreu, J.N., *Parable of the beast* (New York: Macmillan Press, 1968).

Bucaille, M., *The Bible, the Quran, and science.* Translated by D. Pannell Alastair (Elmhurst, New York: Tahrike Tarsile Press, 1995).

Bucke, R.M., *Cosmic consciousness* (New York: E.P. Dalton Press, 1923).

Cardoso, S. H. & Sabbatini, R. M.E. The animal that weeps. In Cardoso, S. H. (Ed.) *Brain and mind*, 16, December 2002- April 2003. <http://www.cerebromente.org.br/indexge_i.htm>.

Cowan, J.M., *A dictionary of modern written Arabic* (London: MacDonald & Evans Ltd., 1974).

Denton, Michael, *Evolution: A theory in crisis* (Adler and Adler Publishers, 1996).

Einstein, Albert, *Cosmic religion* (New York: Covici-Freide Publishers, 1931).

Erikson, Eric, *Childhood and society* (New York: Norton Press, 1963).

Fromm, Erich, *Escape from freedom* (New York: Henry Holt and Co., 1994).

Fromm, E., *The sane society* (Greenwich, CT: Fawcett Premier Book, 1968).

Fromm, E., *Man for himself* (New York: Henry Holt & Co, 1947).

Glasser, W. & Zunin, L.M., "Reality therapy," In Corsini, R., *Current psychotherapies* (Itasca, Illinois: F.E. Peacock Publishers, Inc., 1973).

Hare, Robert D., *Without conscience* (New York: The Guildford Press, 1993).

Horney, Karen, *The neurotic personality of our time* (New York: Norton and Company, Inc., 1964).

Horney, K. *Neurosis and human growth: The struggle toward self-realization* (New York: Norton and Company, Inc., 1950).

Idris, S.J., *The process of Islamization* (Maryland: International Graphics Printing Company, 1977).

Jung, Carl G., *Modern man in search of a soul* (New York: Harcourt, 1933).

Jung, C.J., *Psychology and religions* (New Haven, CT: Yale University Press, 1963).

Khalifa, Rashad, *Quran: The final testament* (Revised Edition II), (Fremont, CA: Universal Unity Press, 2000).

Khouj, Abdullah M., *The relevance of the Quran to human nature* (Washington, D.C.: The Islamic Society, 1986).

Latif, Syed A., *The mind Al-Quran builds* (Hyderabad, India: The Willa Academy, 1971).

Manaster G. & Corsini, R., *Individual psychology: Theory and practice* (Chicago: Adler School of Professional Psychology, 1982).

Maslow, A.H., *The further reaches of human nature* (New York: Viking Press, 1972).

Mercola, J., "Depression and anger affect the immune system," *Journal of Behavioral Medicine*, 24, 2001, 537-555. http://www.sites.mercola.com/2002/jan/19/depression/_anger.htm.

Muller, Alexander, *You shall be a blessing* (San Francisco: The Alfred Adler Institute, 1992).

Nader El-Bizri, "Brethren of purity," The Institute of Ishmaili Studies, http://www.iis.ac.uk/home.asp?l=en

Nasr, Syed, H., *Science and civilization in Islam* (New York: Plum Books, 1968).

Nasr, S. H., An *introduction to Islamic cosmological doctrines* (Albany: State University of New York Press, 1994).

Peck, Scott, *The road less traveled: A new psychology of love, traditional values and spiritual growth* (New York: Touchstone – Simon and Schuster, 1978).

Pieper, Joseph, *The four cardinal virtues* (Notre Dame, IN: University of Notre Dame Press, 1966).

Powell, J., *Why am I afraid to tell you who I am?* (Allen, TX: Thomas More Publishing, 1998).

Qutb, Syed, M., "The Islamic basis of development," *Islam and development,* (Plainfield, IN: Association of Muslim Social Scientists, 1977).

Rogers, C., *On becoming a person* (New York: Houghton Mifflin Company, 1961).

Rosario, T., *The philosophy of life: The pope and the right to life* (Warren, NH: Pro Fratribes Press, 1989).

Royce, J. E., "The internal senses," *Man and his nature: A philosophical psychology* (New York: McGraw-Hill, Inc., 1961).

Rychlak, Joseph. E., *Personality and psychotherapy: A theory-construction approach* (Boston: Houghton Mifflin Company, 1981).

Sahakian, W.S. (Ed.), *Psychology and personality* (Chicago: Rand-McNally Publishing Co., 1997).

Taslaman, C., *The Quran: Unchangeable miracle.* Translated by Ender Gurol (Eden, South Dakota: Nettleberry Publications, 2006).

Valliuddin, M., *The essential features of Islam* (Hyderabad, India: Da'iratu'l Ma'arif Press, no publication date given).

Wood, Garth, *The myth of neurosis* (New York: Harper & Row Publishers, 1986).

Yogananda, P., *The science of religion* (Los Angeles: Self-Realization Fellowship, 2001).

www.ingramcontent.com/pod-product-compliance
Lightning Source LLC
Chambersburg PA
CBHW032056020426
42335CB00011B/363